At Issue

What Should We Eat?

Other Books in the At Issue Series

At Issue

What Should We Eat?

Roman Espejo, Book Editor

GREENHAVEN PRESS
A part of Gale, Cengage Learning

GALE
CENGAGE Learning·

Farmington Hills, Mich • San Francisco • New York • Waterville, Maine
Meriden, Conn • Mason, Ohio • Chicago

Judy Galens, *Manager, Frontlist Acquisitions*

For more information, contact:
Greenhaven Press
27500 Drake Rd.
Farmington Hills, MI 48331-3535
Or you can visit our Internet site at gale.cengage.com

For product information and technology assistance, contact us at

Gale Customer Support, 1-800-877-4253
For permission to use material from this text or product, submit all requests online at www.cengage.com/permissions.

Further permissions questions can be e-mailed to permissionrequest@cengage.com.

Articles in Greenhaven Press anthologies are often edited for length to meet page requirements. In addition, original titles of these works are changed to clearly present the main thesis and to explicitly indicate the author's opinion. Every effort is made to ensure that Greenhaven Press accurately reflects the original intent of the authors. Every effort has been made to trace the owners of copyrighted material.

LIBRARY OF CONGRESS CATALOGING-IN-PUBLICATION DATA

Names: Espejo, Roman, 1977- editor.
Title: What should we eat? / Roman Espejo, book editor.
Description: Farmington Hills, Mich.: Greenhaven Press, a part of Gale, Cengage Learning, [2016] | Series: At issue | Includes bibliographical references and index.
Identifiers: LCCN 2015029477 | ISBN 9780737773903 (hardback) | ISBN 9780737773910 (paperback)
Subjects: LCSH: Nutrition--Juvenile literature. | Health--Juvenile literature. | BISAC: JUVENILE NONFICTION / Health & Daily Living / Diet & Nutrition.
Classification: LCC RA784 .W488 2016 | DDC 613.2--dc23
LC record available at http://lccn.loc.gov/2015029477

Printed in Mexico
1 2 3 4 5 6 7 20 19 18 17 16

Contents

Introduction

Americans have a serious sweet tooth, according to a 2014 study published in *JAMA Internal Medicine*. It found that 71.4 percent of adults consume more than 10 percent of daily calories from added sugars in food and beverages each day. "Consumption of added sugar, including all sugars added in processing or preparing foods, among Americans aged 2 years or older increased from an average of 235 calories per day in 1977–1978 to 318 calories per day in 1994–1996. This change was mainly attributed to the increased consumption of sugar-sweetened beverages,"[1] states the study. Despite decreases in consumption, it purports that Americans have too much of the sweetener: "Although the absolute and percentage of daily calories derived from added sugars declined between 1999–2000 and 2007–2008, consumption of added sugars remained high in US diets, especially among children."[2]

The most pressing issue about sugar is that it's blamed for the rise in worldwide obesity. Similarly, the Harvard T.H. Chan School of Public Health singles out the added sugar in sugar-sweetened beverages as the culprit: "Rising consumption of sugary drinks has been a major contributor to the obesity epidemic."[3] It states that in a twenty-year study of 120,000 men and women, those who added a twelve-ounce serving of a sugary drink to their diets every day "gained more weight over time—on average, an extra pound every 4 years—than people who did not change their intake." The school contends that people "who drink this 'liquid candy' do not feel as full as

---

1. Quanhe Yang et al., "Added Sugar Intake and Cardiovascular Diseases Mortality Among US Adults," *JAMA Internal Medicine*, April 2014. http://archinte .jamanetwork.com/article.aspx?articleid=1819573.
2. Ibid.
3. "Sugary Drinks and Obesity Fact Sheet," Harvard T.H. Chan School of Public Health, accessed July 14, 2015. http://www.hsph.harvard.edu/nutritionsource/sugary-drinks -fact-sheet.

if they had eaten the same calories from solid food and do not compensate by eating less." It is believed that the body has difficulty converting the fructose in sugar into glucose, which is consequently stored as fat. This fat is not used as energy immediately, which accounts for the lack of feeling full and eventual weight gain.

Additionally, sugar is speculated to increase the chance of dying from heart disease. The *JAMA Internal Medicine* study, for example, purported that participants who consumed between 10 to less than 25 percent of calories from sugar had a 30 percent higher risk of heart disease. "[F]or those who consumed 25% or more of calories from added sugar, the relative risk was nearly tripled,"[4] the study warns.

Finally, there's having a sweet tooth and the risk of tooth decay. A 2014 study published in BMC Health concluded that sugar is its only cause. "Only 2% of people at all ages living in Nigeria had tooth decay when their diet contained almost no sugar, around 2g per day. This is in stark contrast to the USA, where 92% of adults have experienced tooth decay,"[5] maintains study author Aubrey Sheiham, emeritus professor of dental public health at University College London.

Action on Sugar, a British group of health experts, argues that people do not need to eat it, period. "Added sugar in our diet is a very recent phenomenon . . . and only occurred when sugar, obtained from sugar cane, beet and corn, became very cheap to produce. No other mammal eats added sugar and there is no requirement for added sugar in the human diet,"[6] it explains. Action on Sugar continues that it is "a totally un-

---

4. Op. cit.
5. University College London, "Dental and Nutrition Experts Call for Radical Rethink on Free Sugars Intake," September 15, 2014. http://www.eurekalert.org/pub_releases /2014-09/ucl-dan091514.php.
6. "Worldwide Experts Unite to Reverse Obesity Epidemic by Forming 'Action on Sugar,'" Consensus Action on Salt and Health, January 9, 2014. http://www .actiononsalt.org.uk/actiononsugar/Press%20Release%20/120017.html.

necessary source of calories" and "gives no feeling of fullness," concurring with the Harvard T.H. Chan School of Public Health.

Nonetheless, the consensus on sugar as highly unhealthy, even toxic, is not unanimous. Bill Shrapnel, deputy chairman of the University of Sydney Nutrition Research Foundation in Australia, contends, "Low sugar is not necessarily good and high sugar is not necessarily bad because sugar isn't the main game." Jennie Brand-Miller, also in the department of nutrition at the University of Sydney, proposes that the focus on the sweetener distracts from the unhealthy excess consumption of fat, salt, and alcohol. "[Sugar] doesn't actually do any direct harm to the human body. It doesn't raise blood cholesterol or raise blood pressure or cause cancer." And concerning the link between increasing obesity and increasing sugar consumption, Brand-Miller remains unconvinced: "Australians have been eating less and less sugar, and rates of obesity have been increasing."[7]

In fact, The Sugar Association declares that sugar is an essential ingredient. "The simple, irrefutable fact is this: sugar is a healthy part of a diet. Carbohydrates, including sugar, are the preferred sources of the body's fuel for brain power, muscle energy and every natural process that goes on in every functioning cell."[8] Furthermore, it disagrees with the argument that sugar is a greater cause of obesity than other substances. "With only 15 calories per teaspoon, sugar is no more fattening than any other 15 calories. Like all carbohydrates, the body converts sugar into fuel quickly. Fats, on the other hand, are stored in fat cells to be used later," explains the association.

---

7. Quoted in Leigh Dayton, "A Spoonful of Sugar Is Not So Bad," *The Australian*, July 9, 2011. http://www.theaustralian.com.au/news/health-science/a-spoonful-of-sugar-is -not-so-bad/story-e6frg8y6-1226090126776.

8. "Balanced Diet," The Sugar Association, accessed July 14, 2015. http://www.sugar.org /sugar-your-diet/balanced-diet.

Of course, sugar is not the only thing to serve up controversy with each serving. Entire diets—such as going organic or gluten-free as seen in recent years—are based on eliminating certain kinds of foods entirely. This anthology, *At Issue: What Should We Eat?*, investigates what foods and ingredients divide nutritionists, activists, researchers, and consumers alike.

1

Top Ten Reasons to Go Organic

Renee Loux

Renee Loux is an expert in sustainability and a chef, television host, author, and columnist for Women's Health Magazine. *She is based in Los Angeles and New York City.*

Regardless of diet, eating organic foods should be prioritized for both personal health and the environment. It is the only way to avoid the hundreds of chemicals used in commercially grown foods—many of which were approved before extensive testing— and genetically modified organisms (GMOs). Because organic foods are grown in soil that is sustainably managed and nourished, they are also more nutritious and delicious. Plus, choosing organic animal products is especially important for children, pregnant women, and nursing mothers to avoid meat and dairy contaminated with hormones, antibiotics, and drugs. Finally, going organic helps to preserve our ecosystems and natural resources, decrease pollution, and support sustainable farming and organic agriculture.

Regardless of diet, organic foods are a smart priority. Opting for organic foods is an effectual choice for personal and planetary health. Buying organically grown food—free of harmful chemicals, bursting with more nutrition, taste, and sustainable sustenance—is a direct vote for immediate health and the hopeful future of generations to come.

Here are the top 10 reasons to choose organic foods today:

1. Avoid chemicals

Eating organically grown foods is the only way to avoid the cocktail of chemical poisons present in commercially grown food. More than 600 active chemicals are registered for agricultural use in America, to the tune of billions of pounds annually. The average application equates to about 16 pounds of chemical pesticides per person every year. Many of these chemicals were approved by the Environmental Protection Agency (EPA) before extensive diet testing.

Organically grown foods have more nutrients ... than commercially grown foods because the soil is managed and nourished with sustainable practices by responsible standards.

The National Academy of Sciences reports that 90% of the chemicals applied to foods have not been tested for long-term health effects before being deemed "safe." Further, the FDA tests only 1% of foods for pesticide residue. The most dangerous and toxic pesticides require special testing methods, which are rarely if ever employed by the FDA.

2. Benefit from more nutrients

Organically grown foods have more nutrients—vitamins, minerals, enzymes, and micronutrients—than commercially grown foods because the soil is managed and nourished with sustainable practices by responsible standards. The *Journal of Alternative and Complementary Medicine* conducted a review of 41 published studies comparing the nutritional value of organically grown and conventionally grown fruits, vegetables, and grains and concluded that there are significantly more of several nutrients in organic foods crops.

Further, the study verifies that five servings of organically grown vegetables (such as lettuce, spinach, carrots, potatoes, and cabbage) provide an adequate allowance of vitamin C, whereas the same number of servings of conventionally grown vegetables do not.

On average, organically grown foods provide: 21.1% more iron (than their conventional counterparts); 27% more vitamin C; 29.3% more magnesium; 13.6% more phosphorus.

3. Enjoy better taste

Try it! Organically grown foods generally taste better because nourished, well balanced soil produces healthy, strong plants. This is especially true with heirloom varieties, which are cultivated for taste over appearance.

4. Avoid GMO

Genetically engineered (GE) food and genetically modified organisms (GMO) are contaminating our food supply at an alarming rate, with repercussions beyond understanding. GMO foods do not have to be labeled in America. Because organically grown food cannot be genetically modified in any way, choosing organic is the only way to be sure that foods that have been genetically engineered stay out of your diet.

5. Avoid hormones, antibiotics and drugs in animal products

Conventional meat and dairy are the highest risk foods for contamination by harmful substances. More than 90% of the pesticides Americans consume are found in the fat and tissue of meat and dairy products.

Europe's scientific community agrees that there is no acceptably safe level for daily intake of any of the hormones currently used in the United States and has subsequently banned all growth hormones.

The EPA reports that a majority of pesticide intake comes from meat, poultry, fish, eggs, and dairy products because these foods are all high on the food chain. For instance, a large fish that eats a smaller fish that eats even smaller fish accumulates all of the toxins of the chain, especially in fatty tissue. Cows, chickens, and pigs are fed animal parts, by-products, fish meal, and grains that are heavily and collectively laden with toxins and chemicals. Lower-fat animal products are less dangerous, as toxins and chemicals are accumulated and concentrated in fatty tissue.

Antibiotics, drugs, and growth hormones are also directly passed into meat and dairy products. Tens of millions of pounds of antibiotics are used in animal feed every year. The union of concerned scientists estimates that roughly 70% of antibiotics produced in the United States are fed to animals for nontherapeutic purposes. US farmers have been giving sex hormones and growth hormones to cattle to artificially increase the amount of meat and milk the cattle produce without requiring extra feed. The hormones fed to cows cannot be broken down, even at high temperatures. Therefore they remain in complete form and pass directly into the consumer's diet when meat is eaten.

Hormone supplementation is the biggest concern with beef, dairy products, and farmed fish. In the United States, the jury is still out. However, Europe's scientific community agrees that there is no acceptably safe level for daily intake of any of the hormones currently used in the United States and has subsequently banned all growth hormones.

The major concerns for US consumers include the early onset of puberty, growth of tumors, heightened cancer risks, and genetic problems. Growth hormones in milk (rBGH or rBST) are genetically modified and have been directly linked to cancer, especially in women.

Many scientists and experts warn that rampant use of antibiotics in animal feed, like penicillin and tetracycline, will breed an epidemic that medicine has no defense against. Karim Ahmed, PhD, a senior scientist at the Natural Resources Defense Council (NRDC) states that it "is perhaps one of the most serious public health problems the country faces. We're talking about rendering many of the most important antibiotics ineffective."

Choosing organic animal products is unyieldingly important, especially for children, pregnant women, and nursing mothers.

6. Preserve our ecosystems

Organic farming supports eco-sustenance, or farming in harmony with nature.

Preservation of soil and crop rotation keep farmland healthy, and chemical abstinence preserves the ecosystem. Wildlife, insects, frogs, birds, and soil organisms are able to play their roles in the tapestry of ecology, and we are able to play ours, without interference or compromise.

7. Reduce pollution and protect water and soil

Agricultural chemicals, pesticides, and fertilizers are contaminating our environment, poisoning our precious water supplies, and destroying the value of fertile farmland. Certified organic standards do not permit the use of toxic chemicals in farming and require responsible management of healthy soil and biodiversity.

Leaning heavily on one or two varieties of a given food is a formula for devastation.

According to Cornell entomologist David Pimentel, it is estimated that only 0.1% of applied pesticides reach the target pests. The bulk of pesticides (99%) is left to impact the environment.

8. Preserve agricultural diversity

The rampant loss of species occurring today is a major environmental concern. It is estimated that 75% of the genetic diversity of agricultural crops has been lost in the last century. Leaning heavily on one or two varieties of a given food is a formula for devastation. For instance, consider that only a handful of varieties of potatoes dominate the current market-place, whereas thousands of varieties were once available.

Now, dig back to recent history's potato famine in Ireland, where a blight knocked out the whole crop, which consisted of just a few varieties, and millions of people died of starvation. Today, most industrial farms also grow just one crop rather than an array of crops on one piece of land. Ignorance is bliss? Or amnesia is disastrous? Crop rotation is a simple and effective technique used in organic agriculture to reduce the need for pesticides and improve soil fertility.

Most conventional food is also extremely hybridized to produce large, attractive specimens, rather than a variety of indigenous strains that are tolerant to regional conditions such as droughts and pests. Many organic farms grow an assorted range of food, taking natural elements and time-tested tradition into account. Diversity is critical to survival.

9. Support farming directly

Buying organic food is an investment in a cost-effective future. Commercial and conventional farming is heavily subsidized with tax dollars in America. A study at Cornell University determined the cost of a head of commercial iceberg lettuce, typically purchased at 49 cents a head, to be more than $3.00 a head when hidden costs were revealed. The study factored in the hidden costs of federal subsidies, pesticide regulation and testing, and hazardous waste and cleanup.

Every year, American tax dollars subsidize billions of dollars for a farm bill that heavily favors commercial agribusiness. Peeling back another layer of the modern farming onion reveals a price tag that cannot be accurately measured but certainly includes other detrimental associated costs such as health problems, environmental damage, and the loss and extinction of wildlife and ecology.

10. Keep our children and future safe

Putting our money where our mouths are is a powerful position to take in the $1 trillion food industry market in

America. Spending dollars in the organic sector is a direct vote for a sustainable future for the many generations to come.

2

Eating Organic May Be Harmful

Doug Smith

Doug Smith is the cofounder of True Nutrition, a dietary supplement and nutrition company based in Vista, California.

Eating organically grown produce is healthier than eating fruits and vegetables that are conventionally grown. Nonetheless, what's labeled "organic" at most grocery store chains is farmed with organic pesticides and "growth promoters." While these chemicals are not synthetic, this does not mean they are less harmful; about half of organic pesticides are carcinogenic, for instance. Also, some organic farmers may use up to ten times more of an organic pesticide than a conventional farmer uses a synthetic one. To further protect their choice to eat only organic, consumers should ask grocers questions about their organic produce and grow their own food.

What!? How can this be?

"I switched to only eating organic fruits and vegetables years ago and feel so much better doing so."

How can it be harmful? Organically produced fruits and vegetables are grown in an environment absent of synthetic chemicals, pesticides, unnecessary machinery, chemical growth promoters, poisoned earth/dirt and the like. "Right?"

Well unfortunately, no, not exactly. . . .

I usually get this frantic response when I start off a conversation like the title. Most usually go on this self-pat on the back mentality about how they're in the know or understand eating organically is inherently more healthy than eating conventionally grown vegetables and fruits. Based on what they're told, they're 100 percent correct. You don't need to be a rocket scientist (or a nutritionist for that matter) to know eating something that isn't sprayed with chemicals—and is allowed to grow in a natural environment—is more healthy than eating a conventionally grown fruit or vegetable.

Organic farmers use pesticides and "growth promoters" and are putting more emphasis on their bottom line than they're telling you.

I know a heated conversation can be had on eating organically or eating conventionally grown food, but I'm not here to dispel organic over standard convention farming though, or the pros and cons of each. I'm in the "you are what you eat and I don't want to eat a chemical shit storm of pesticides and growth promoters" boat, regardless of whether or not they're deemed by the government as "safe."

"Okay, so why are you talking trash about my beloved organic veggies? I just took down a full head of kale for lunch and I'm happy as a clam I did so."

The idea of organically grown produce to me (and the majority of other people) is an easy one—what's marketed to us is essentially that they're seeds/plants grown without the use of chemicals, pesticides and growth promoters.

But what if I were to tell you the majority of "organically" grown produce is not absent of any of these very things that conventional farmers use? Organic farmers use pesticides and "growth promoters" and are putting more emphasis on their bottom line than they're telling you. The truth is there's a ton of money in selling organic produce and the powers that be know this. You'd think in theory without all the additional chemicals and steps of conventional farming the price would be cheaper to grow a less processed produce, no? But the reality is in most cases all of the conventional farming techniques are used on organic produce.

Before we get into the specifics below, I definitely want to point out, this is in no way a smear piece about why you should stop eating organically grown produce.

These are a few words put together to hopefully push for some change in the direction organically grown produce is headed.

The idea of growing food in absence of man-made chemicals or any chemicals for that matter is essential for our public health, I do fully believe that. Although I feel Americans—or any person for that matter—want to do what's right and will go above and beyond to do the right thing, we also can get pretty lazy and allow large corporations and government agencies to dictate and direct what we want to see.

You made the choice to eat only organic and that's great, but you must go a few steps further to protect this decision.

Just because it's a "natural" pesticide, that doesn't necessarily mean it's better or even good for you at all.

So what about the chemicals? The reality is, the majority of organically grown produce—especially the stuff you see in most grocery store chains—is most likely grown with pesticides. The fact is, most state laws allow organic farmers to spray a whole gamut of chemical sprays, powders and pellets on their organic crops. That is, if they are "organic" or natural chemical sprays, powders and pellets.

So what the hell does organic mean then these days? It means that organically produced fruits and vegetables are grown in an environment absent of synthetic chemicals, yes, but the notion that they're grown without chemicals at all is false.

Pesticides can be used in the growing of "organic" vegetables and fruits, and often are. They just must be derived from natural sources, not synthetically manufactured.

So my question to you is, in all the knowledge in your head, is this any better? It isn't to me, and some major U.S. organizations would agree. Just because it's a "natural" pesticide, that doesn't necessarily mean it's better or even good for you at all.

The EPA and USDA have conducted many studies over the last few decades showing synthetically used pesticides, or any chemical for that matter, are seriously carcinogenic—a little more than 50 percent of them. A carcinogen leads to a high susceptibility for cancer creation within the human body. So again, it seems it's fairly logical to not use any of these chemicals ("natural" or not) anywhere near our foods.

But what about these organic pesticides?

Not until very recently has anyone tested or cared to test these natural organic pesticides, mainly for the thought that they are "natural" so why test them, how harmful can they be? Guess what happened when they tested these natural pesticides—the very pesticides they're using on our organic produce? About half of them are carcinogenic as well. Yikes.

So I guess the question is, are natural pesticides less harmful and/or toxic than synthetically derived ones? That's a super difficult question to answer considering not much testing has been done and for good reason. The organic market is a fairly new one and with everyone jumping on the wagon and bending the rules of the USDA, FDA and EPA, there are so many variables.

Here's a very common practice in growing lettuce: In conventional farming, during the full growth cycle of this plant, a very small amount of a very well-tested pesticide (literally tested over 50 years) will be used once, maybe twice to assure a healthy crop. But for an organic farmer, they might use five to 10 times more of a natural pesticide like rotenone-pyrethrin or Spinosad. Tests done by the USDA have shown pesticides are 10 times more prevalent on organic lettuce than on conventionally grown produce in some cases.

Economics and money can sometimes pull the wool so quickly over our eyes, you'd think we were at a sheep farm.

There's also the question of farming and our environment. We've seen the repercussions of our actions and decisions as humans the last few hundred years and we've really started to ask questions about what kind of impact our farming and the feeding of our species is doing to our world's environment. You'd think less chemicals, natural or not, is better for the environment. But if these organic farmers are spraying considerably more of these natural chemicals than conventional farmers, is that really any better? That natural pesticide mentioned above, rotenone-pyrethrin, is extremely toxic to aquatic life and fish. So which is better?

As I stated earlier, this isn't a grouping of words to discourage you from continuing on your quest to a cleaner lifestyle by utilizing organically grown produce. It's for the eye-opening reality of what's currently happening and, in return, that you'll be empowered to demand better.

I don't blame the farmer, I don't blame the associations that regulate organic foods and I certainly don't blame our government.

The reality is we're in a capitalist society—in some ways it's what makes this country so great—but it also comes with dire reactions if we don't remain aware. Economics and money can sometimes pull the wool so quickly over our eyes, you'd think we were at a sheep farm. Although I'm not saying it's right or wrong, it seems money and economics will always come first. I don't doubt that if a farmer could make the same amount of money from an apple grown without anything in *true* organic style, they'd do so.

On the flip-side if they know they can use a certain natural chemical to assure a strong, non-pest effected crop, and still state that it's "organically grown," they're going to continue doing that as well.

"Okay, that kale I just had for lunch doesn't feel so good after all, so what do I do?"

The answer is a very easy one, it takes us opening our mouth and asking questions. We can ask our grocer about the organic produce we're buying—who's the grower and where did it come from? I can almost guarantee any organic produce item we buy that's perfectly packaged in a plastic container or plastic bag is most likely from a huge producer, one that also produces conventionally grown produce (they're all in on the fun, there's money in those organic hills). Again, I'm not an economist or a horticulturalist, but I'd guess they'd be using organic pesticides, it just makes smart business sense.

Besides being that guy asking questions at our grocery store, an even better solution is buying local. The local farm stand and farmers' market movement is huge these days. Besides keeping our hard earned money local and helping our fellow farmers, we're also most likely greatly helping your health. We get to talk directly to the farmer and can ask them about what, if anything, they spray or add to their produce.

More times than most, the local organic farmers are organically farming the way you'd think organic farming should be, as in the absence of chemicals of any kind.

We need to take things into our own hands, literally.

We can grow something organic with our own dirt and two hands. Even if it's in a small pot on our window sill, we can all *farm* on some level. We can learn what it takes (not much) to create our own food virtually free. Just a little hard work and time is all we need.

Want to go even further? Find a plot of land in your neighborhood that isn't being used and ask the owner or the township/city if you can use it for a community garden—the possibilities are really endless.

Growing one's food is an amazing way to connect ourselves to the very sustenance that keeps us alive. I can almost guarantee this connection will inspire you to speak out louder on the current state of organic farming and crops.

3

Eating Red Meat Is Not a Healthy Choice

Eugenia Killoran

Eugenia Killoran is the food and fitness journalist for the Pritikin Program in Miami, Florida.

A recent Harvard study was misconstrued by the media as concluding that unprocessed red meats such as beef, lamb, and pork are not harmful to eat. However, all meats have saturated fat and cholesterol, and consuming them in large amounts is proven to raise bad cholesterol. Also, there is growing evidence that the increased intake of heme iron and iron stores through red meats heightens the risk of heart disease, type-2 diabetes, and some types of cancer. Furthermore, grilling, frying, and broiling meat creates carcinogens and other unhealthy substances. As for the Harvard study, it was observational, not controlled, inaccurately assessing what the subjects actually ate.

Recently America was atwitter over red meat.

A new study from Harvard found that each two-ounce increase in daily consumption of processed meats like bacon, hot dogs, and cold cuts was associated with a 42% greater risk of heart disease and 19% heightened chance of diabetes.

But, unfortunately, what got most of the headlines was the news on *unprocessed* red meats like beef, lamb, and pork. They were not linked with more heart disease or diabetes in this study.

And here's what America heard: "Just in time for summer ... chow down! Red meat is good for you!" newscasts announced, sporting images of outdoor grills jammed with sizzling steaks. Newspapers had headlines like "guilt-free hamburgers."

"Baloney," warned Jay Kenney, PhD, who has been studying the link between diet and increased risk of disease for the past four decades and is Nutrition Research Specialist at the Pritikin Longevity Center in Miami, Florida.

Unless 1 + 1 no longer equals 2, it would be beyond naive to suggest that increasing meat intake would NOT increase coronary heart disease.

"While the media correctly reported that this study added to evidence that processed meats, loaded with salt and other damaging ingredients, are particularly unhealthy, it grossly misinterpreted the study's findings on unprocessed meat. Never did this study say that eating red meat like burgers and steak was okay."

Not a License to Eat Red Meat

The lead author of the new study, Renata Micha, PhD, agreed. In an interview with *Pritikin Perspective*, the Harvard research fellow stated: "It is very important to stress that unprocessed red meat was not associated with LOWER risk of heart disease and diabetes. Therefore, people should not use these findings as license to eat as much unprocessed red meats as they like." Rather, "they should give more emphasis to increasing intake in their diet of foods that have been shown to be protective, such as fruits, vegetables, whole grains, fish, and nuts." Yes, Dr. Micha echoes the Pritikin Eating Plan.

And the media, admonished Dr. Kenney, should give more emphasis to science that is irrefutable. "It is proven beyond any doubt that increasing saturated fat and cholesterol in the diet raises 'bad' LDL [low-density lipoprotein] cholesterol levels in the blood, and *all* meats have some saturated fat and cholesterol. Obviously, fatty cuts are worse, but even unprocessed lean meat, especially if consumed in large amounts, will raise LDL cholesterol.

"There is also irrefutable evidence linking elevated LDL cholesterol levels to increased atherosclerosis, the underlying cause of most heart attacks and strokes in the U.S. Unless 1 + 1 no longer equals 2, it would be beyond naive to suggest that increasing meat intake would *NOT* increase coronary heart disease."

Keep in mind, too, that there is growing evidence linking increased heme iron intake and iron stores, the result of increased red meat consumption, with heightened risk of developing not only heart disease and type 2 diabetes but also several types of cancer.

"There is also a growing body of data showing that high-temperature cooking of meat, especially grilling, frying, and broiling, generates a variety of known and suspected carcinogens as well as other troubling substances like advanced glycation end products (AGEs) that may also promote vascular disease, diabetes, and/or cancer," pointed out Dr. Kenney.

What we don't know from this study is the total amount of saturated fat and cholesterol that people consumed.

Key Concerns

Now, back to the study that got all the press last week. Published online in *Circulation*, it was an analysis of previously published studies, called a meta-analysis.

Here is one key concern: The studies the Harvard researchers reviewed were observational studies, *not* controlled clinical trials. "Observational studies," explained Dr. Kenney, "are notoriously inaccurate at assessing what people actually ate. Such data hardly refute much better quality data from clinical trials.

"Controlled clinical trials, the gold standard of scientific research, have proven a strong and consistent link between eating more red meat and elevated LDL cholesterol levels, and between higher LDL levels and more coronary heart disease."

Here's another example of how observational studies can sometimes steer us in the wrong direction. Most have not found an association between salt intake and blood pressure, but numerous clinical trials have clearly shown that the more salt we eat, the greater our risk of high blood pressure, strokes, and heart disease.

There's one other key issue that needs to be raised regarding this study's claims about red meat and disease. To begin, let's assume that the data were accurate, that people did in fact report the correct amount of meat they were eating. We'll then assume the conclusions were correct: When the scientists compared those who ate steak and other unprocessed red meat with those who ate less (on average, four ounces less per day), they came up empty. Heart disease risk was the same.

But what we *don't* know from this study is the *total* amount of saturated fat and cholesterol that people consumed. It is quite likely that the people who ate *less* red meat ate *more* dairy, poultry, and other foods high in saturated fat and cholesterol. If they did, they could have ended up eating *similar* amounts of saturated fat and cholesterol as the heavy meat eaters, and having *similar* cholesterol profiles and *similar* risks of heart disease. We will never know because this meta-analysis did not look at total amounts of saturated fat and cholesterol in people's diets. But it's certainly a valid question given food trends in America over the past 40 years. Since 1970, beef consumption has dipped considerably while chicken and some dairy products (especially cheese, which is very high in saturated fat) have shot up. Since 1970, the average American has *tripled* his cheese consumption. That's a lot of saturated fat. And very likely, a lot of clogged arteries.

Ounce for ounce, cheeses like cheddar and monterey have about three times as much saturated fat as ground beef. Three times!

Replacing Burgers with Chicken McNuggets

The point here is: You can cut a lot of red meat out of your diet, maybe even get rid of it completely, "but it will not likely reduce your LDL cholesterol or heart disease risk if you're replacing your steak and burgers with Chicken McNuggets and cheese omelets," points out Dr. Kenney. "Now, you *would* reduce your LDL cholesterol and heart attack risk if instead of steak and burgers you were choosing meatless chili and veggie burgers because that switch would in fact reduce your intake of saturated fat and cholesterol."

And when it comes to red meat, you're certainly far better off choosing lean, low-in-saturated-fat cuts like the grass-fed bison steak served at the Pritikin Longevity Center than fattier cuts, especially fatty processed meats like bacon, bologna, hot dogs, ham, and sausages. But even then, bison is a once-a-week choice, not an every-night choice, because it still has some saturated fat and cholesterol. If you eat large quantities of *any* food containing saturated fat and cholesterol, your LDL cholesterol is bound to go up, and with it, your risk of heart disease.

Sensational Headlines, Not Accurate Analysis

The new Harvard study concluded that just a *little bit* of processed meat, each additional two-ounce serving consumed daily, was linked with significant increases in heart and diabetes risk. Processed meat, with its high salt content and larger amounts of other additives, is particularly unhealthy.

This study also looked at the risk of heart disease and diabetes for each additional four-ounce serving of unprocessed meat consumed daily. It did not find a statistically significant association. Translated: Red meat was not linked with raised risk, but it was not linked with lower risk either.

What this study did *not* show, but what many media reports erroneously inferred, is that eating lots of unprocessed red meat was perfectly fine; it would not increase our risk of heart disease or diabetes. These reports, more intent on sensational headlines than on accurate analysis, left many people thinking, "Let's fire up the BBQ. Let's pile on the pork chops and steaks." What a tragedy.

4

Red Meat Should Be Eaten in Moderation

Rochelle Bilow

Rochelle Bilow is the associate editor of Bon Appétit *magazine.*

The scientific evidence says that red meat is good—and bad—for you. Many studies throughout the decades claim that it is harmful to cardiovascular health, particularly processed meats, and vegetarians have the lowest incidences of ischemic heart disease. Furthermore, others report that excessive red meat consumption is linked to a variety of cancers. In fact, according to a 2009 study, eating four ounces of it a day increased a person's chance of dying in ten years by 30 percent. Other research, however, purports that high-protein "caveman" diets decrease bad cholesterol levels and lower weight. Given the conflicting nature of the scientific evidence, it is wise for people to practice moderation when eating red meat.

We know that red meat tastes great, and that's reason enough for us to dig into a medium-rare steak with gusto. But in the last few decades, there's been as much talk about its health benefits and/or risks as its flavor. Either red meat will lower your cholesterol and help you slim down (some studies say), or it'll set you on the fast track to diabetes, heart disease, and cancer (according to other studies). What's a diner to do? Before you swap that sirloin for shiitakes, hang on just a moment. We're looking to find an answer once and for all: Is beef good for you or bad for you? What does science say about red meat?

It'll Stop Your Heart! Or Maybe Not!

One of the biggest complaints about red meat is that it's bad for your cardiovascular health. In 1999, a study that compared heart disease in vegetarians, regular meat eaters, and occasional meat eaters found that vegetarians experienced the lowest rates of ischemic heart disease (hardening of the arteries). But another study conducted that year claimed that because saturated fats are to blame for heart disease, meat-eaters can happily live in health—so long as they consume leaner cuts. Shortly after, in 2000, the Weston A. Price Foundation spoke out against the red-meat naysayers, claiming that it's not steak and lamb chops but refined carbohydrates and vegetable oils that are actually the cause of heart disease.

We'll be on the safe side if we keep the franks and charcuterie to a minimum—and stay away from the grill. In essence: practice moderation.

In 2004, research showed that women who consume excessive red meat are more likely to contract type-2 diabetes. Add that to a study conducted in 2009, which found that those who consumed red meat (beef, lamb, and pork, according to the researchers) were 30 percent more likely to die of heart disease and cancer. Instead of cutting out meat completely, the researchers suggested baking and poaching the meat rather than grilling or frying it. It would seem that if we just cut back on the burgers and poached our hot dogs, we'd be in the clear. . . .

It wasn't that simple, though, because a study in 2013 cited L-carnitine, a compound found in red meat, as the culprit. L-carnitine was proven to be devoured by bacteria that live in the gut, then converted to trimethylamine-N-oxide, a compound that has, in turn, been proven to clog arteries—in mice, anyway. Although L-carnitine is found in plenty of foods, like asparagus and ice cream, there's a much higher concentration in meats like beef, pork, and lamb. The redder the meat, the greater amount of L-carnitine; 4 ounces of cooked ground beef contains 87–99 milligrams of the compound, more than 20 times what you'd find in a 1/2 cup of whole milk.

But wait. In June 2014, a study found that the dangers of red meat—heart failure and death in particular—were aggravated by *processed* red meat, like sausages and hot dogs. According to the study, men who consumed over 75 grams of processed red meat a day were 28 times more likely to suffer heart failure than men who ate less than 25 grams daily. For a little frame of reference, an Oscar Mayer all-beef hot dog clocks in at about 45 grams. So if we're taking these findings for rote, we'll be on the safe side if we keep the franks and charcuterie to a minimum—and stay away from the grill. In essence: practice moderation.

It's (Possibly) a Cancer-Causer

Our cardiovascular systems aren't the only thing at risk, according to research. Scientists have been studying the effects of red meat on various cancers, as well. In 1996, it was reported that women age 55 to 69 who consumed red meat "frequently" were more likely to develop lymph node cancer. Interestingly, a fact sheet about the correlation between meat consumption and breast cancer, published in 2000, found that studies implicating red meat have proven mostly inconclusive—instead, eating *more* vegetables and fruits was touted as a more effective way to prevent breast cancer.

In 2007, the American Institute for Cancer Research found that certain cancers—lung, pancreas, and stomach, to name a few—were *possibly* caused by excessive red meat consumption.

The meta-analysis of previously published studies explains, "Eating meat may be associated with an increased risk of breast cancer, but, owing to differences in the results and design of studies examining this question, it is not possible to be sure about this risk." The connection between colorectal cancer and processed red meat high in saturated fat appeared to have been proven by the most extensive research, including a 2005 study that found that limiting red meats would likely decrease the colorectal cancer risk. In an editorial about the study, Walter Willet of the Harvard School of Public Health wrote, "Fortunately, substituting pistachio-encrusted salmon and gingered brown basmati pilaf for roast beef with mashed potatoes and gravy is not a culinary sacrifice."

Back in 2003, another study found that "very low" intake of meat—less than one serving a week—actually increased life expectancy.

Then in 2007, haem, the pigment in hemoglobin, was thought to have possibly been a contributing factor to red meat's connection with colon cancer. In 2010, however, a critical summary of previous studies asserted that due to certain Western lifestyle factors—smoking, obesity, low intake of fiber and high consumption of alcohol and refined sugar—the connection implicating red meat as a cause of colon cancer wasn't sound enough to back.

It'll Just Kill You. Maybe.

As if all of that wasn't scary enough, a study in 2009 made waves when it stated that regular consumption of beef and pork caused increased early mortality rates. And this wasn't some minor study of a few hundred people eating whole smoked briskets. No, according to the *Washington Post*, it followed more than half a million "middle-aged and elderly Americans" and "found that those who consumed about four ounces of red meat a day (the equivalent of about a small hamburger) were more than 30 percent more likely to die during the 10 years they were followed, mostly from heart disease and cancer." Even worse, the *Post* wrote, "Sausage, cold cuts and other processed meats also increased the risk."

Another extensive study on the matter in 2012 reaffirmed the hypothesis: Excessive consumption of red meat (over 42 grams a day, according to the researchers) correlated to increased mortality rates. But not everyone bought the findings. British nutritionist and obesity researcher Zoë Harcombe took the study to task in a blog post that outlined potential problems, including the facts that one of the researchers is a vegetarian (potential conflict of interest, she argues) and that we're all actually going to die someday—regardless of what we eat. By the way, back in 2003, another study found that "very low" intake of meat—less than one serving a week—actually *increased* life expectancy. So, uh, yeah.

But the Cavemen Loved It!
(Didn't They Die Young?)

The paleolithic diet is officially a *thing*, but people have been eating like cavemen for years. The Atkins diet, a popular low-carb diet that focused on consumption of proteins and fats, sparked a flurry of controversy when it swept the nation in the late 1990s. Although a high-protein diet isn't composed exclusively of red meat (dieters are encouraged to eat chicken, fish, cheese, and vegetables, too), if you're nixing carbs in favor of animal protein, chances are you'll be eating a lot more steak.

There's been some positive talk about a meaty diet: in 2002, it was found that a high-protein Atkins-style diet decreased cholesterol levels and lowered weight—one of the original intents of Atkins. A subsequent study in 2003 also found evidence that an Atkins diet increased good cholesterol levels while lowering those of bad cholesterol.

In 2010, however, a study claimed that Atkins dieters experience increased "all-cause" mortality rates, despite their potentially lower cholesterol. In 2012, a study claimed that women who ate high-protein diets, like Atkins, increased their risk of stroke and heart disease by 28 percent. The paleo diet has come under fire, too. *Scientific American* in 2013 explained that while many paleo dieters claim eating plenty of red meat protects them from "modern" diseases like cancer, the impracticality of eating like a caveman in modern day renders the argument null. In 2014, research suggested that high-protein diets were as harmful to health as smoking and likely to cause cancer and diabetes (in people under 65, so seniors, eat up!) It's also been noted that although cavemen didn't get diabetes and heart disease, they also rarely lived long enough to develop those issues.

While we're not going to give up our burgers, steaks, meatballs, and chops, there's also something to be said for a little moderation.

Was This Always Such a Big Deal?

We've been debating the health benefits and consequences of red meat for years in the public sphere, although the focus on specific ramifications, like cancer and high cholesterol, are a more recent topic of intrigue: In the early 1900s, much of the chatter around red meat revolved around a general state of wellbeing. In 1892, for example, the *New York Times* reported that an ideal summertime diet for a man of "ordinary size, doing ordinary physical or mental work," included (among other things) 4 ounces of steak for breakfast, 2–3 ounces of beef, mutton, or lamb for lunch, and 3–4 ounces of "any red meat."

On a speedier news day in 1904, readers were encouraged to eat less beef, mutton, and pork—and although that was because meat processors and packers were striking, the editorial did argue that "Everybody knows that the average American harms himself by including an oversupply of red meat in his daily ration." Also making the case for moderation in all things meat, a report about a steel worker who had fallen ill in 1925 outlines the man's recovery plan for a clean bill of health: In addition to limiting his wife's pie and ice cream, getting plenty of sleep, and following "the Golden Rule," he was advised to eat red meat just once a week. After three weeks of this diet, he declared himself to be "as hale and hearty as any other eighty-year-old man anywhere." Surely, we all aspire to his example.

So Should I Eat This Steak or Not?

All this drama is a headache—it's enough to have us reaching for a bottle of red wine (though *that's* another story). With two clear camps pitted against each other, we're finding ourselves situated, well, somewhere in the middle. While we're not going to give up our burgers, steaks, meatballs, and chops, there's also something to be said for a little moderation. After all, with so much good-for-you and delicious food to be cooked and eaten, we're not about to give up *anything* completely. Life's just too—well—short.

5

Fish: Friend or Foe?

Harvard T.H. Chan School of Public Health

The Harvard T.H. Chan School of Public Health is a professional graduate school of Harvard University.

As a low saturated fat source of nutrients like omega-3 fatty acids and vitamin D, fish is a very important part of a healthy diet. But less than one in five Americans eats the recommended amount. Many worry that mercury, pesticide residues, and other contaminants found in fish and seafood can be harmful. However, overall, increased consumption would prevent many more deaths from heart disease than cause cancer deaths, and other foods contain similar levels of mercury and other contaminants. Eating a variety of fish and seafood is an easy way to avoid these contaminants. Women who are pregnant and nursing should still eat fish regularly, but avoid certain types.

Fish is a very important part of a healthy diet. Fish and other seafood are the major sources of healthful long-chain omega-3 fats and are also rich in other nutrients such as vitamin D and selenium, high in protein, and low in saturated fat. There is strong evidence that eating fish or taking fish oil is good for the heart and blood vessels. An analysis of 20 studies involving hundreds of thousands of participants indicates that eating approximately one to two 3-ounce servings of fatty fish a week—salmon, herring, mackerel, anchovies, or sardines—reduces the risk of dying from heart disease by 36 percent.[1]

Harvard T.H. Chan School of Public Health, "Fish: Friend or Foe?" The Nutrition Source, Dept. of Nutrition, Harvard School of Public Health, 2014. www.hsph.harvard.edu/nutritionsource/fish/. Copyright © 2008 Harvard University. All rights reserved. Reproduced with permission.

Eating fish fights heart disease in several ways. The omega-3 fats in fish protect the heart against the development of erratic and potentially deadly cardiac rhythm disturbances. They also lower blood pressure and heart rate, improve blood vessel function, and, at higher doses, lower triglycerides and may ease inflammation. The strong and consistent evidence for benefits is such that the Dietary Guidelines for Americans, the American Heart Association, and others suggest that everyone eat fish twice a week.[2, 3]

[The] levels of PCBs and dioxins in fish are very low, similar to levels in meats, dairy products, and eggs.

Unfortunately, fewer than one in five Americans heeds that advice. About one-third of Americans eat seafood once a week, while nearly half eat fish only occasionally or not at all.[4] Although some people may simply not like fish, the generally low consumption is likely also caused by other factors, including perceptions about cost, access to stores that sell fish, and uncertainty about how to prepare or cook fish. Still others may avoid seafood because they worry that they—or their children—will be harmed by mercury, pesticide residues, or other possible toxins that are in some types of fish.

Should you forgo fish because of the contaminants they might carry? It's a controversial topic that is often fueled more by emotion than by fact. Here's what's known about the benefits and risks of eating fish and other seafood:

- *Known or likely benefits*: In a comprehensive analysis of human studies, Harvard School of Public Health professors Dariush Mozaffarian and Eric Rimm calculated that eating about 2 grams per week of omega-3 fatty acids in fish, equal to about one or two servings of fatty fish a week, reduces the chances of dying from heart disease by more than one-third.[1] Both observational studies and controlled trials have also demonstrated that the omega-3 fats in fish are important for optimal development of a baby's brain and nervous system, and that the children of women who consume lower amounts of fish or omega-3's during pregnancy and breast-feeding have evidence of delayed brain development.

- *Possible benefits*: Eating fish once or twice a week may also reduce the risk of stroke, depression, Alzheimer's disease, and other chronic conditions.[11]

- *Possible risks*: Numerous pollutants make their way into the foods we eat, from fruits and vegetables to eggs and meat. Fish are no exception. The contaminants of most concern today are mercury, polychlorinated biphenyls (PCBs), dioxins, and pesticide residues. Very high levels of mercury can damage nerves in adults and disrupt development of the brain and nervous system in a fetus or young child. The effect of the far lower levels of mercury currently found in fish are controversial. They have been linked to subtle changes in nervous system development and a possible increased risk of cardiovascular disease. The case for PCBs and dioxins isn't so clear. A comprehensive report on the benefits and risks of eating fish compiled by the Institute of Medicine calls the risk of cancer from PCBs "overrated."[5]

Striking a Balance

Avoiding fish is certainly one way to avoid mercury or PCBs. But is that the wisest choice, given the benefits of eating fish? Drs. Mozaffarian and Rimm put this in perspective in their analysis in the *Journal of the American Medical Association*.[1] First, reviewing data from the Environmental Protection Agency and elsewhere, they calculated that if 100,000 people ate farmed salmon twice a week for 70 years, the extra PCB intake could potentially cause 24 extra deaths from cancer—

but would prevent at least 7,000 deaths from heart disease. Second, levels of PCBs and dioxins in fish are very low, similar to levels in meats, dairy products, and eggs. Third, more than 90 percent of the PCBs and dioxins in the U.S. food supply come from such non-seafood sources, including meats, dairy, eggs, and vegetables. So, given these limited health effects, low levels in fish, and major sources from other foods, the levels of PCBs and dioxins in fish should not influence your decision about which fish to eat (just as it does not influence your decision about whether or not to eat vegetables, meats, dairy products, or eggs, the major sources of PCBs and dioxins). One exception: if you eat local freshwater fish caught by friends or family, it makes sense to consult local advisories about the amounts of such fish you should eat.

Women should recognize that avoiding seafood altogether is likely to harm their babies' brain development.

At the levels commonly consumed from fish, there is also limited and conflicting evidence for effects of mercury in adults; thus, the Environmental Protection Agency, the Food and Drug Administration, the Institutes of Medicine report, and the analysis by Mozaffarian and Rimm all conclude that this evidence is insufficient to recommend limitations on fish intake in adults, given the established benefits of fish consumption for cardiovascular disease. In fact, the easiest way to avoid concern about contaminants is simply to eat a variety of fish and other seafood.

Except perhaps for a few fish species, the scale tips in favor of fish consumption for women who are pregnant. High intake of mercury appears to hamper a baby's brain development.[6] But low intake of omega-3 fats from fish is at least as dangerous. In a study of almost 12,000 pregnant women, children born to those who ate less than two servings of fish a week didn't do as well on tests of intelligence, behavior, and development as children born to mothers who ate fish at least twice a week.[7] A study conducted by Harvard researchers showed that visual recognition scores in six-month-olds were highest in those whose mothers ate at least two servings of fish a week during pregnancy but who also had low mercury levels.[8] Several other observational studies of fish intake during pregnancy, and randomized controlled trials of fish oil during pregnancy or breast feeding, have found similar benefits of mothers' fish or fish oil intake for their babies' brain development.

So, women should recognize that avoiding seafood altogether is likely to harm their babies' brain development. The healthiest approach for women who are or may become pregnant, nursing mothers, and young children is to eat two servings per week of fish or other seafood, including up to one serving per week of white (albacore) canned tuna, and avoid the four fish species higher in mercury (shark, swordfish, tilefish, king mackerel). It is important that women recognize that the list of fish and seafood that they should eat is far larger than the few specific species to be avoided. Here's what the Environmental Protection Agency and Food and Drug Administration recommend for women who are or may become pregnant, nursing mothers, and young children:

- Don't eat shark, swordfish, king mackerel, or tilefish (sometimes called golden bass or golden snapper) because they contain high levels of mercury.

- Eat up to 12 ounces (two average meals) a week of a variety of fish and shellfish that are lower in mercury. Shrimp, canned light tuna, salmon, pollock, and catfish are low-mercury fish. Albacore ("white") tuna has more mercury than canned light tuna. So limit your intake of albacore tuna to once a week. You can find a table of various fish, their omega-3 fatty acid content, and their average load of mercury and other contaminants online in the article by Mozaffarian and Rimm.[1]

- Check local advisories about the safety of fish caught by family and friends in your local lakes, rivers, and coastal areas. If no advice is available, eat up to 6 ounces (one average meal) per week of fish you catch from local waters, but don't consume any other fish during that week.

- So, these recommendations emphasize that women who are or may become pregnant, nursing mothers, and young children should eat fish, avoiding only four specific (and generally rarely consumed) fish species. Importantly, the latter limitation does not apply to the rest of the population, for whom the evidence supports simply choosing a variety of fish and seafood.

What If You Hate Fish?

Not all omega-3 fats come from fish. In fact, Americans also consume plant omega-3s in the form of alpha-linolenic acid (ALA), which is found in flax seeds, walnuts, and a few vegetable oils. In the human body, ALA is not converted to the marine omega-3s, EPA and DHA, to any large extent. So, the evidence does not support eating ALA as a replacement for seafood consumption. On the other hand, some data from observational studies like the Nurses' Health Study suggest that getting extra ALA may reduce the chances of cardiovascular disease.[9] Another analysis, from the Health Professionals Follow-up Study, showed that higher intake of ALA may be particularly important for protection against heart disease in people who didn't eat much fish.[10] Since these findings haven't yet been replicated in randomized trials, the exact benefit of ALA is still a bit up in the air, but eating more foods rich in this good fat may also be good for health.

References

1. Mozaffarian D, Rimm EB. Fish intake, contaminants, and human health: evaluating the risks and the benefits. *JAMA.* 2006; 296:1885-99.

2. U.S. Dept. of Health and Human Services USDA. Dietary Guidelines for Americans, 2005. Washington, D.C., 2005.

3. Kris-Etherton PM, Harris WS, Appel LJ. Fish consumption, fish oil, omega-3 fatty acids, and cardiovascular disease. *Circulation.* 2002; 106:2747-57.

4. Attitudes and Beliefs About Eating Fish: A National Opinion Survey Conducted for The Center for Food, Nutrition and Agriculture Policy.

5. Seafood Choices: Balancing Risks and Benefits. Institute of Medicine: Washington, D.C., 2007.

6. Grandjean P, Weihe P, White RF, et al. Cognitive deficit in 7-year-old children with prenatal exposure to methylmercury. *Neurotoxicol Teratol.* 1997; 19:417-28.

7. Hibbeln JR, Davis JM, Steer C, et al. Maternal seafood consumption in pregnancy and neurodevelopmental outcomes in childhood (ALSPAC study): an observational cohort study. *Lancet.* 2007; 369:578-85.

8. Oken E, Wright RO, Kleinman KP, et al. Maternal fish consumption, hair mercury, and infant cognition in a U.S. Cohort. *Environ Health Perspect.* 2005; 113:1376-80.

9. Albert CM, Oh K, Whang W, et al. Dietary alpha-linolenic acid intake and risk of sudden cardiac death and coronary heart disease. *Circulation.* 2005; 112:3232-8.

10. Mozaffarian D, Ascherio A, Hu FB, et al. Interplay between different polyunsaturated fatty acids and risk of coronary heart disease in men. *Circulation.* 2005; 111:157-64.

11. Raji CA, Erikson KI, Lopez OL, Kuller LH, Gach HM, Thompson PM, Riverol M, Becker JT. Regular fish consumption and age-related brain gray matter loss. *Am J. of Prev Med.* 2014; 47(4):444-51.

6

People Should Not Eat More Fish

Environmental Working Group

Headquartered in Washington, DC, the Environmental Working Group is a nonprofit, nonpartisan organization dedicated to protecting human health and the environment.

The US Food and Drug Administration (FDA) released new guidelines for eating fish and seafood, encouraging everyone—including pregnant and nursing women—to significantly increase their consumption. While high in beneficial omega-3 fatty acids, iodine, and vitamin D, some species are also high in contaminants—especially mercury—and a blanket recommendation such as the FDA's is inadequate. Not all people would benefit from eating more, such as vegetarians and those who eat healthfully. Furthermore, not all consumers are aware that fish and seafood are not equally nutritious or which ones to eat. It is recommended that people limit their consumption to two to three meals per week, or else the benefits decrease and the risks of contaminants increase.

In June of this year [2014] the federal Food and Drug Administration [FDA] and Environmental Protection Agency [EPA] proposed new guidelines that encourage pregnant and nursing women to consume eight to 12 ounces of a variety of seafood per week, choosing from varieties lower in mercury.

The FDA/EPA proposal represented a significant change from the agencies' 2004 guidelines, which advised pregnant women, those who might become pregnant and nursing mothers to eat *no more than 12 ounces* of low-mercury seafood.

This time around, the agencies set a floor as well as a ceiling on seafood consumption. They recommend that pregnant women, those who might become pregnant and nursing mothers boost their intake of fish dramatically from 3.6 ounces per week, the current national average, to eight to 12 ounces weekly. They said young children should eat more fish, the amount dependent on their weight and age. This advice echoed the [President Barack] Obama administration's Dietary Guidelines for Americans, published in January 2011, which said all adults should eat eight to 12 ounces of "a variety of seafood types."

Large predatory fish, including tuna, shark, marlin and swordfish, which eat smaller fish, accumulate considerable mercury over life spans that may run decades.

The basis for this recommendation is research indicating that "good fats," particularly polyunsaturated omega-3 fatty acids, offer extraordinary and unique health benefits.

The two most beneficial omega-3 fatty acids—docosahexaenoic acid, known as DHA, and eicosapentaenoic acid, known as EPA—have been shown to reduce inflammation and severity of heart and retinal diseases. Children born to mothers who ate low-mercury seafood during pregnancy experienced better functioning brain and nervous systems. They scored two to six points higher on intelligence tests than children whose mothers ate little fish during pregnancy. A diet rich in omega-3s lowered blood triglycerols, reduced arrhythmias and decreased the risk of sudden death from heart disease.

Fish and shellfish are low in fat, high in protein and good sources of iodine, vitamin D and selenium, often deficient in the Western diet. But decades of industrial activity, particularly emissions from coal-fired power plants, have released mercury and other pollutants into oceans and waterways. Those contaminants end up in seafood. While most commercial fish and shellfish contain some mercury, concentrations vary depending on the fishes' ages, diet, region of harvest and other factors. Large predatory fish, including tuna, shark, marlin and swordfish, which eat smaller fish, accumulate considerable mercury over life spans that may run decades.

Omega-3 concentrations vary widely among species but are typically highest in species that dwell in cold water and have oily flesh. Some fish species are high in mercury but low in omega-3s. Others have higher concentrations of omega-3s with very little mercury.

EWG [Environmental Working Group] strongly agrees with the administration's Dietary Guidelines for Americans when it calls for Americans to eat more fruits and vegetables, high-fiber whole grains and seafood, and to eat less sugar, solid fat, refined grains and sodium. However we disagree with the blanket recommendation that all adults aim to eat 8 to 12 ounces of seafood per week. Many people are at low risk for heart disease, including vegetarians and other adults with an otherwise healthy diet. If all Americans followed the federal government's advice, the amount of seafood consumed in the U.S. could triple, and global fisheries could suffer.

High-risk populations—pregnant women, children and people with heart disease—are likely to benefit from eating more seafood, *provided* they select varieties with the least mercury and optimum omega-3 content. To do so they need specific and detailed information about omega-3s and mercury content of common varieties.

EWG's investigation of government and scientific data on seafood contamination and omega-3 content has found that seafood varied widely on both counts. We conclude that the federal government's approach, advising Americans to "eat more fish and to eat a variety of fish from choices that are lower in mercury," is inadequate. The reasons: shoppers may not know that some commercial species likely to contain less mercury are also very low in omega-3 fatty acids.

People who eat lots of fish or shellfish should pay attention to local seafood advisories and select only low-mercury species.

In an analysis released earlier this year, EWG cautioned that not everyone who follows the government's dietary guidelines and eats two or three meals per week would achieve the intended health benefits. This is a particular concern for pregnant women and young children who eat fish higher in mercury. Our analysis found that:

10 to 35 common commercial species have too much mercury for women of average weight to eat twice weekly during pregnancy.

19 of the 35 have too much mercury for children.

The proposed FDA/EPA advisory urges pregnant women and children to avoid four species—swordfish, tilefish, king mackerel and shark. EWG goes further, recommending that people also limit their consumption of a larger number of moderate-mercury species.

Not all fish are equally nutritious. Twenty-one of the 35 common fish and shellfish we investigated would not provide an adequate amount of omega-3s when eaten twice weekly. This includes most fish and shellfish species often found in the American diet.

Dangerous substances besides mercury can build up in fish and shellfish. Among them are dioxin and other persistent pollutants. While these pollutants are generally less harmful than mercury, their presence is a reminder that people who eat lots of fish or shellfish should pay attention to local seafood advisories and select only low-mercury species.

EWG recommends that people restrict their seafood consumption to two or three meals per week. Beyond that amount, the beneficial effects of omega-3s subside and the risks posed by contaminants add up.

How Do You Know You're Eating Enough Seafood and the Right Seafood?

It all depends on who you are, your age, your pregnancy status and your health.

IF YOU ARE CONSIDERING GETTING PREGNANT, ARE PREGNANT OR NURSING

Federal nutrition guidelines recommend that you consume an average of 250 milligrams daily of DHA and EPA, the two omega-3 fatty acids found primarily in seafood. The most critical period is the last 10 weeks of pregnancy.

Not all seafood species are equal. One to two servings of a high-omega-3 species like salmon, sardines or Pacific or Atlantic mackerel can meet the weekly recommendation for omega-3s. But a pregnant woman would need to eat five or more servings of tilapia, shrimp or catfish to get the optimum amount of omega-3s.

Because mercury from seafood can linger in your body, you should limit your mercury consumption before you conceive, or soon in pregnancy. Mercury can pass through breast milk. It is wise to continue avoiding higher-mercury fish while breastfeeding.

IF YOU ARE FEEDING CHILDREN

Children benefit from eating seafood but should consume smaller portions. Always serve low-mercury seafood. Children should eat no more than one serving of canned light tuna per week. Children should never eat canned albacore tuna, also known as white tuna.

IF YOU HAVE BEEN DIAGNOSED WITH HEART DISEASE

The Obama administration's Dietary Guidelines for Americans report "moderate evidence" that consumption of two servings of seafood weekly can reduce the number of deaths from heart attacks and strokes. But eating more than two meals a week does not appear to offer additional benefits.

Some studies of people who ate large quantities of fish or species high in mercury have reported neurological and other health problems.

On the other hand, eating high-mercury fish can erode some cardiac benefits of seafood. For this reason, people with heart disease should make an effort to limit their exposure to mercury.

IF YOU ARE AT LOW RISK FOR HEART DISEASE AND NOT PREGNANT

For most adults, seafood is beneficial but not essential.

Adults who eat fish frequently, particularly those who eat sushi, recreationally-caught fish or high-mercury fish, are at risk for mercury toxicity. Some studies of people who ate large quantities of fish or species high in mercury have reported neurological and other health problems.

IF YOU EAT FISH OR SHELLFISH CAUGHT FROM LOCAL WATERWAYS

Many streams and rivers are contaminated with mercury and other pollutants from industrial pollution. Locally caught fish can sometimes be more polluted than those purchased in stores. State and local governments have issued dozens of location-specific warnings and guidelines for taking fish and shellfish from polluted lakes and streams. Check the U.S. Environmental Protection Agency's searchable webpage for fish advisories by state, or check your state's website for information about local waterways. When a local waterway is not the subject of a specific advisory, the FDA/EPA advisory recommends that adults eat no more than six ounces and children, one to three ounces, of any non-commercial fish and seafood per week.

IF YOU LOVE SUSHI AND EAT IT FREQUENTLY

People who eat sushi weekly, particularly high-mercury types such as tuna, are at risk for excessive mercury, according to a survey of more than 1,000 New Yorkers and New Jerseyans by scientists at Rutgers University. Tuna in sushi had three to 10 times more mercury than eel, crab, salmon and kelp rolls. Tuna served at upscale sushi restaurants and prepared as sashimi and nigiri had the highest mercury concentrations of all. Tuna in maki rolls sold at supermarkets and less expensive restaurants had lower mercury levels. The Rutgers study calculated that the 10 percent of respondents who ate the most sushi would ingest roughly triple the recommended daily intake for mercury.

Pregnant women who don't eat fish can find omega-3 fatty acids in fish oils, fortified foods and omega-3 supplements.

Many common sushi varieties are made from overharvested fish species. Check Monterey Bay Aquarium's Sushi Guide for sustainability ratings.

IF YOU EAT CANNED TUNA

Americans eat more than 400 million pounds of canned imported tuna because it is affordable and can be stored for a long time. Albacore tuna, also called "white" tuna, contains significant amounts of omega-3s but also significant mercury contamination. "Light" tuna is usually skipjack tuna but can also be yellowfin or tongol tuna. These varieties have lower mercury levels than albacore but fewer omega-3s.

The June FDA/EPA advisory recommended that pregnant women limit their consumption of albacore tuna to six ounces weekly. EWG is more cautious: we recommend that children, pregnant women and nursing mothers eat no more than two servings of albacore tuna per month, with the exact quantity depending on age and weight.

The June FDA/EPA advisory said canned light tuna was relatively lower in mercury. We disagree. EWG recommends no more than one serving per week of light tuna for children and two servings for pregnant or nursing women.

IF YOU DON'T EAT SEAFOOD

Omega-3s are important during pregnancy and early childhood. But these fats are not as necessary for other adults, provided they eat an otherwise healthy diet. Pregnant women who don't eat fish can find omega-3 fatty acids in fish oils, fortified foods and omega-3 supplements.

Oils containing the important omega-3 fatty acids DHA and EPA can be made from a variety of seafood species or extracted from algae. In general, dietary supplements are poorly regulated, so consumers cannot determine the supplements' true omega-3 content. Nor can they be sure mercury or other contaminants are not present. Few data are available on this problem. Concentrations of mercury and other contaminants in supplements appear to be low and vary depending on the species of fish that serve as the basis for the particular supplement. Consumer Labs tests of fish oils sold in the U.S. found none with more than 0.01 parts per million mercury; in other words, a dose of a supplement contained less mercury than a single serving of most fish.

Some milk, eggs and margarines are fortified with DHA. Others foods, including canola oil, soybean oil, flax seeds, chia seeds and walnuts contain a third type of omega-3 fat known as alpha-lineoic acid or ALA, which the body can convert to

DHA and EPA. However, people generally convert less than 10 percent of the ALA in their diet to EPA, which is then converted to DHA. This makes ALA consumption a less effective source of good fats, and less reliable option during pregnancy.

If you buy foods that claim to be fortified with omega-3s, check the product labels for DHA and ALA. (No foods are supplemented with EPA.) Nutritional guidelines suggest that women consume 250 milligrams of DHA and EPA daily during pregnancy. Many foods contain far less.

The U.S. government's Medline database rates fish oil supplements as "effective" for people with high triglycerides and "likely effective" for people with heart disease. But fish oil supplements are rated only as "possibly effective" treatments for many other health conditions, including arthritis, stroke, osteoporosis, age-related eye disease and attention deficit-hyperactivity disorder.

There is no reliable scientific evidence that pregnant women and nursing mothers who take omega-3 supplements have infants who enjoy benefits in growth, neurodevelopment and vision comparable to women who ate seafood during pregnancy.

Fish oil supplements appear to be slightly less beneficial for cardiac patients than a seafood-rich diet, perhaps because seafood has important trace nutrients like iodine, vitamin D, vitamin B12 and selenium. As well, people who eat seafood are probably less inclined to eat unhealthy proteins like fatty or highly processed meats.

EWG recommends that women who are pregnant and anyone at risk for cardiac disease consult their physicians if they do not eat seafood frequently to discuss other ways to add omega-3s to their diets.

7

People Should Not Eat Fast Food

Joseph Mercola

Joseph Mercola is an osteopathic physician, advocate of alternative medicine, and founder of Mercola.com.

If McDonald's itself advised employees to avoid eating its burgers and fries, people should avoid eating fast food. Of course, such fare cannot be considered "real food"—fast food items are heavily processed, which destroys nutrients and loads them with unhealthy additives, leading to many modern diseases and conditions. For instance, french fries are full of the worst fats that exist, and McDonald's McRib sandwich contains a chemical found in sneakers. One study, in fact, demonstrates that eating fast food twice a week can lead to a ten-pound weight gain and double the risk of insulin resistance. Consequently, people should focus on raw, fresh foods and forgo fast food altogether.

McDonald's is the poster child for the modern Western diet and all the health problems that it engenders. As a general rule, "food" was designed to supply your body with all the nutrients it needs.

Processing destroys many of the nutrients and is the primary contribution to most of the chronic degenerative diseases many experience today. I would also argue that food processed to the point of not decomposing after more than a decade is not actually *real food* and shouldn't be consumed. . . .

Ironically, the fast food giant recently ended up with a PR [public relations] nightmare after suggesting its own employees forgo fast food fare for healthier options like salad and water. As reported by *Business Insider*:

> Several excerpts from the posts, which were created from a third-party vendor, warned against the negative effects of fast food, even going so far as labeling a cheeseburger and fries, core items on its menu, as an "unhealthy choice."

The site also warned employees that fast-food meals are "almost always high" in calories, fat, sugar, and salt—and rightfully so, I might add. Warning employees of the health hazards of the very food they produce and serve, however, does not make for good PR.

You might be asking yourself why you're being forced to subsidize fast food profits, especially when you consider that such foods are at the heart of our current health crisis.

In response to the controversy, McDonald's shut down the website in question, which was aimed at providing "work and life advice" to employees. According to a company spokesman, the information was "taken out of context," thereby generating "unwarranted scrutiny and inappropriate commentary." Employees will still be able to receive work and life advice over the phone.

Is Fast Food Giant Skirting Social Responsibilities?

McDonald's has received a variety of unflattering attention lately. Last month, fast food workers around the US rallied in protest of low wages, demanding the hourly wage to be raised to $15 per hour.

At present, the average fast food worker makes less than $9 per hour, and according to a recent study by the University of Illinois at Urbana-Champaign, more than 50 percent of US fast food workers are enrolled in some form of public assistance program, costing US tax payers an estimated $7 billion annually.

You might be asking yourself why you're being forced to subsidize fast food profits, especially when you consider that such foods are at the heart of our current health crisis. . . .

Contrary to popular belief, nearly 70 percent of fast food workers are actually adults, and the main wage earners in their family. Gone are the days when fast food joints were staffed primarily with high school students. This too, I believe, is a sign of how the food culture has changed in this country.

Fast food restaurants are a primary source of food for a lot of people these days. British chef Jamie Oliver is but one vocal "real food" advocate who addresses this issue head-on, pointing out that our food culture has changed so drastically over the last 30 years that a majority of today's youth do not even know what fresh, whole food is.

Fast food restaurant work is also full-time employment—if not a career, albeit a poor-paying one—for many. Case in point: Nancy Salgado, a single mother, claims she still makes $8.25 after working for McDonald's for a decade! The following video went viral last October, when Salgado was threatened with arrest for shouting out a protest during a talk given by McDonald's president Jeff Stratton.

> *"It's really hard for me to feed my two kids and struggle day to day. Do you think this is fair, that I have to be making $8.25 when I have worked for McDonald's for 10 years?"* she shouts.

How Government Farm Subsidies Have Created a Disease-Ridden Country

There's little doubt that the Western diet, high in ultra-processed food, is a major source of many of our modern diseases. McDonald's and other fast food restaurants are not necessarily the root of the problem, though. They're simply an outgrowth of the food system created and upheld by the US government. . . .

This is a recipe for obesity, diabetes, and heart disease, just to name a few of the conditions that commonly befall those who consume "the Standard American Diet."

US food subsidies are grossly skewed toward factory-farmed meats, grains, and sugars, with very little fresh fruits and vegetables or healthy fats from nuts and seeds. What you end up with when you get paid to mass produce those ingredients is a cheap fast food diet. . . .

The fact that a hamburger can be had for less than an organic salad is a major contributing factor to why fast food is consumed as frequently as it is. The same goes for soda, loaded with cheap high fructose corn syrup (HFCS), compared to a bottle of plain water.

Needless to say, if your diet consists of burgers and super-size sodas, your meals may be cheap, but it is also excessively high in grains, sugars, and factory-farmed meats. This is a recipe for obesity, diabetes, and heart disease, just to name a few of the conditions that commonly befall those who consume "the Standard American Diet."

Tellingly, in contrast to third-world countries, in the US, higher rates of obesity is actually linked to poverty, suggesting that the American "poor man's diet" (which tends to be exceptionally high in processed foods and fast food) has a drastic and adverse impact on your metabolism. Indeed, many on the most limited food budgets, such as those who receive food assistance dollars, live in "food deserts"—areas without grocery stores, and perhaps only a convenience store or a fast-food restaurant where they can purchase their food.

The Food Lobby Wields Great Power over Public Health

Thanks to the tireless efforts of the powerful food lobby, Congress keeps subsidizing foods that we really should be eating LESS of—including factory farmed meats and corn (which ends up as HFCS that is used in nearly every single processed food and sweet beverage on the market.) The farm bill also has a direct impact on what your child gets fed in school, and what food assistance programs will distribute to poorer households.

I believe many of our society's chronic health problems could be resolved if attention was paid, at the highest levels of government, to the root problem—our agricultural subsidies. If growers of subsidized fresh vegetables were in a clear majority, you might start to see some fine advertising campaigns promoting the consumption of those veggies.

Unfortunately, the Department of Agriculture is deeply entrenched with the agri-business, and current legislations protect the profits of these large industries at the expense of public health. Sadly, you also see this influence in nutrition science. It is actually not designed to help you make sound dietary choices but rather to allow food companies to make health claims to increase profits, and this is a primary reason why you cannot get sound dietary advice from the US government.

Eating dietary fat isn't what's making you pack on the pounds. It's the sugar/fructose and grains that are adding the padding.

Processed Food Contains Many Potentially Dangerous Ingredients

I've written numerous articles highlighting the hazards of specific fast food fare, and why such heavily processed foods cannot be considered "real food." This includes:

- Chicken McNuggets, which have made it into mainstream news on a number of occasions because of the potentially hazardous additives they contain.

- Soda can contain any number of health harming substances, from high fructose corn syrup (HFCS) to benzene and aspartame.

- French fries are loaded with the worst types of fat on the planet—typically highly refined and genetically modified omega-6 oils, such as corn, canola and soybean oils.

- Thankfully, the FDA [Food and Drug Administration] recently announced it may remove trans fats found in margarine, vegetable shortening, and partially hydrogenated vegetable oils from the list of "generally recognized as safe" (GRAS) ingredients. This would be the first step toward ridding the American diet of this harmful fat.

- McDonald's seasonally-available McRib sandwich contains more than 70 ingredients, including a chemical used in gym shoes. And the pork is actually a restructured meat product made from the less expensive innards and scraps from the pig.

It's quite clear that fast food leads to obesity and insulin resistance. As demonstrated in one 15-year long study, eating fast food just *twice* a week can make you gain 10 pounds and *double* your risk of developing insulin resistance, compared to eating it less than once a week. The bottom line is that if you want to stay healthy, and keep your children healthy, you have to avoid fast food and other processed foods, and invest some time in your kitchen, cooking from scratch.

What Makes for a Healthy Diet?

I firmly believe that the primary keys for successful weight management and optimal health are:

1. Severely restricting carbohydrates (refined sugars, fructose, and grains) in your diet

2. Increasing healthy fat consumption

3. Unlimited consumption of non starchy vegetables. Because they are so low calorie, the majority of the food on your plate will be vegetables

4. Limit the use of protein to less than one half gram per pound of body weight

---

I don't think fast food companies like McDonald's are as clueless about the health impact of their food as they would like you to believe.

Healthful fat can be rich in calories, but these calories will *not* affect your body in the same way as calories from non-vegetable carbs. As explained by Dr. Robert Lustig, fructose in particular is "isocaloric but not isometabolic." This means you can have the same amount of calories from fructose or glucose, fructose and protein, or fructose and fat, but the *metabolic effect* will be entirely different despite the identical calorie count. Eating dietary fat isn't what's making you pack on the pounds. It's the sugar/fructose and grains that are adding the padding.

So please, don't fall for the low-fat myth, as this too is a factor in the rise in chronic health problems such as heart disease and Alzheimer's. Your brain, heart, and cardiovascular system *need* healthy fat for optimal functioning. In fact, emerging evidence suggests most people need at least half of their daily calories from healthy fat, and possibly as high as 85 percent. My personal diet is about 70–80 percent healthy fat. Add to that a small to medium amount of high-quality protein and plenty of vegetables. You actually need *very few* carbs besides vegetables. However, by volume the largest portion of my plate is clearly vegetables.

Take Control of Your Diet and Your Health

I don't think fast food companies like McDonald's are as clueless about the health impact of their food as they would like you to believe. And advising their employees to forgo fast food fare and soda for more wholesome food is indeed good advice. The thing is, it's advice that applies to every single one of their customers as well. . . . Healthy eating is actually far easier than most people think. Here's a quick and dirty summary: if you're new to healthful living, these four basic steps can put you on the right path toward vastly improved health, regardless of what your government's dietary guidelines are:

- Focus on raw, fresh foods, and avoid as many processed foods as possible (for those who still have trouble understanding what "processed food" is: if it comes in a can, bottle, or package, and has a list of ingredients, it's processed)

- Avoid foods that contain fructose (check the label for ingredients like corn syrup or high fructose corn syrup)

- Limit or eliminate grain carbohydrates, and replace them with healthful fats, such as avocados, butter made from raw grass-fed organic milk, grass-fed meats, and organic pastured eggs, coconuts and coconut oil, and raw nuts such as macadamia

- Replace sodas and other sweetened beverages with clean, pure water

8

New Fast-Food Restaurants Offer Healthy Menus

Shan Li

Shan Li reports on the restaurant and retail industries for the Los Angeles Times.

Rather than cooking up unhealthy burgers or fried chicken, the fastest-growing fast-food chain restaurants offer healthy meals, responding to the nation's growing interest in locally sourced, wholesome food. Putting grass-fed beef and kale banana smoothies on the menus, these entrepreneurs aim to balance the offerings of very good but expensive restaurants with healthy "cheap eats." Of course, high-quality ingredients come at a higher cost, and these fast-food chains do not offer any "dollar menu" equivalent. But entrepreneurs of these chains believe that consumers are willing to pay a little more for convenient food that's good for them.

Some of the fastest-growing fast-food chains aren't slinging artery-clogging cheeseburgers or cooking up calorie-packed fried chicken.

Instead, diners can order Brussels sprouts salads and kale smoothies, served with the same speed as In-N-Out or Burger King.

America's interest in locally sourced and healthy foods has spurred a boom in farmers markets and farm-to-table restaurants and has expanded organic produce at the supermarket.

Now, a number of upstart chains trying to tap that interest are taking aim at traditional fast food by moving leafy greens and fruits to the center of the plate.

These rapidly expanding restaurants want to revolutionize the fast-food industry, bringing healthy fare to the masses who typically don't shop at Whole Foods. At the same time, they are stealing customers from stalwarts such as McDonald's.

The most bankable word in food service is fresh.

These chains, several based in California, see a juicy opportunity in the Golden State, with its bounty of health-obsessed diners interested in the latest food fads.

The "Bankable Word" in Food

Such chains make up just a tiny fraction of the $200-billion fast-food industry in the United States. But analysts predict this sector will boom as health conscious consumers ditch the burger and fries in favor of quickly prepared healthy meals.

"The most bankable word in food service is fresh," said restaurant consultant Aaron Allen.

Many are rethinking the fast-food experience beyond food. At some, you'll find real china replacing paper dishes and foam cups for in-house eating. There are cushy chairs and communal tables, not plastic ones that are nailed down. Several offer beers from local breweries and menus that change with the seasons.

"People want to eat more vegetables that are nutritious and unprocessed," said Greg Dollarhyde, chief executive of Santa Monica-based chain Veggie Grill. "The big trend now is make it better for me, but I don't want to give any flavors up."

Many of these restaurants cater to salad skeptics or meat lovers who shy away from anything green or overly healthy.

"I don't like saying the H word because that's going to turn people off," said Mike Donahue, co-founder of Lyfe

Kitchen, which has expanded to 13 locations since opening its first restaurant in Palo Alto in 2011. "I tell our people they have got to start every message with, 'Tastes great, tastes great, tastes great. And oh, by the way, it is good for you.'"

Lyfe Kitchen serves burgers with grass-fed beef and decadent chocolate desserts, all under 600 calories. Donahue said the company avoids pushing the uber-healthy aspects of its dishes—focusing on the tastiness of its kale banana smoothies, for instance, instead of highlighting the kale.

Even Veggie Grill, which offers only vegetarian food, sells meatless cheeseburgers and chicken wings to entice "recovering carnivores," Dollarhyde said.

A Balance Between Expensive Restaurants and Cheap Eats

The popularity of chains that offer quick yet healthy meals is driven by millennials who grew up watching the Food Network and aging baby boomers who want to maintain their health.

"Younger consumers eat out a lot, and they don't want to feel bad about their choices every day," said Kelly Weikel, senior consumer research manager at Technomic Inc., a food industry consulting firm. "Eating healthy is also appealing for boomers. When they eat out, they go for a little bit healthier because they are trying to preserve their vitality."

Zsofi Paterson, 29, said she avoids traditional fast-food joints and used to depend on sushi and the salad bar at Whole Foods for quick meals. The corporate advisor from Santa Monica said she dines at least once a week at chains such as Simply Salad or Tender Greens.

"I like getting something tasty and not greasy and horrible for you," Paterson said. "You can also sit down because it's an actual restaurant."

Several of the healthy chain founders did time at conventional eateries. Donahue of Lyfe Kitchen logged two decades at McDonald's. The three founders of Tender Greens met while working at the luxurious Shutters on the Beach in Santa Monica, where two served as chefs.

Although McDonald's and other chains have been trying to increase their healthy offerings, many of their menu items remain laden with calories, saturated fat and sodium.

"We wanted to find a balance between the very expensive but very good restaurant world we spent our careers in, and the mom-and-pop cheap eats that we could afford but weren't really in line with our lifestyle," said Erik Oberholtzer, chief executive of Tender Greens.

Although McDonald's and other chains have been trying to increase their healthy offerings, many of their menu items remain laden with calories, saturated fat and sodium.

For example, the popular McDonald's double cheeseburger weighs in at 430 calories, 10 grams of saturated fat and 1,040 milligrams of sodium. A small order of fries adds 230 calories, 1.5 grams of saturated fat and 130 milligrams of sodium.

Lyfe Kitchen sells a grass-fed beef burger with 544 calories, 8 grams of saturated fat and 635 milligrams of sodium. But those watching their figures can opt for the marinated kale at a svelte 68 calories, 1 gram of fat and 74 milligrams of sodium. The quinoa crunch bowl contains 552 calories, 3 grams of saturated fat and 551 milligrams of sodium.

Quickly Expanding

Cost is another difference. The double cheeseburger is a stalwart on McDonald's Dollar Menu; nothing is that cheap at the chains that promote themselves as health centered.

High-quality ingredients can pose a challenge for these chains, which need to find reliable suppliers while quickly expanding.

Tender Greens operates 17 locations, all in California. It so far has partnered with Scarborough Farms in Oxnard for most of its produce.

Now with an eye toward eventually expanding outside the Golden State, the Culver City chain plans to experiment with modern farming techniques that will enable it to grow food in indoor spaces such as abandoned industrial buildings.

"That will allow us to not only scale up but also to scale our produce, take it on the road, and bring the farm with us," Oberholtzer said.

These quick health-food spots are finding strong demand for not only finer ingredients but also extra dining frills that add to the overall experience.

At Lyfe Kitchen, which plans to open up to 20 locations next year [2015], waiters deliver meals; diners order at the counter and then are handed a GPS device so they can be easily located inside the restaurant. Food is served on real china with flatware and glasses.

Sweetgreen, which is opening in West Hollywood and Santa Monica next year, has branched outside of restaurants by throwing an annual music and food festival called Sweet-Life.

Co-founder Nathaniel Ru said Washington, D.C.-based Sweetgreen is working to improve its app so customers can order food as well as pay for meals on their mobile devices. Frequent app users are invited to enjoy perks such as special dinners and festival tickets.

Diners Willing to Pay More for Good Meals

The entrepreneurs behind healthy fast food say they are confident that diners will be eager to pay slightly more for good meals that are easy on the arteries.

"What you saw in the past with fast food was all convenience," said Cameron Lewis, co-founder of Simply Salad. "Now we can make healthy, good-quality food in the same time as your typical fast-food experience."

He and partner Bruce Teichman opened their first Simply Salad in 2010 after emptying out their savings accounts. In August, their third location opened in Santa Monica.

They plan to add five restaurants in the L.A. area in the next two years and then take on the rest of the state and beyond. The restaurants have thrived, especially with diners who want to get in and out in less than 30 minutes without downing a burrito or burger.

"If you want to go to McDonald's or Burger King, obviously feel free," Teichman said. "But you get what you pay for."

9

Six Truths About a Gluten-Free Diet

Consumer Reports

Consumer Reports is a nonprofit organization that aims to empower and create a safe marketplace for consumers. It publishes the monthly magazine Consumer Reports.

While gluten is blamed for a number of conditions, going gluten-free as a diet trend may not be beneficial. Removing the protein means more added sugar and fat, so many gluten-free foods are less nutritious. Going gluten-free may increase exposure to arsenic due to the increased consumption of rice products. It may lead to weight gain due to the higher calories, sugar, and fats in gluten-free foods. They are also more expensive—food manufacturers incur extra costs for certification and labeling. Avoiding gluten without a proper diagnosis may conceal other health problems or reactions to another food. Last but not least, because of cross contamination, many gluten-free foods may not be gluten-free.

Eighteen months ago [in May 2014], Ahmed Yearwood decided to go gluten-free. "A few years earlier, I'd given up processed foods and felt great," the 41-year-old business owner recalls. "I figured cutting out gluten would make me feel even better. Everyone told me I'd have more energy and lose weight." He lasted less than a month. "Everything was rice this and rice that—it was way too restrictive," he says. "And I didn't feel any different healthwise than I did before." Yearwood reverted to his former eating habits. "Some of the grains I eat have gluten, but I still feel amazing."

Just as fat was vilified in the 1990s and carbs have been scorned more recently, gluten—a protein found in wheat, barley, and rye—has become the latest dietary villain, blamed for everything from forgetfulness to joint pain to weight gain. "Gluten free" is a claim you see on everything from potato chips to bread to hummus—and even on cosmetics and laundry detergent. Some people must avoid the protein because they have celiac disease—an autoimmune condition in which gluten causes potentially life-threatening intestinal damage—or gluten sensitivity. But less than 7 percent of Americans have those conditions.

A recent Consumer Reports review of 81 products free of gluten across 12 categories revealed that they're a mixed bag in terms of nutrition.

According to a recent survey of more than 1,000 Americans by the Consumer Reports National Research Center, 63 percent thought that following a gluten-free diet would improve physical or mental health. About a third said they buy gluten-free products or try to avoid gluten. Among the top benefits they cited were better digestion and gastrointestinal function, healthy weight loss, increased energy, lower cholesterol, and a stronger immune system.

Yet there's very limited research to substantiate any of those beliefs, notes Alessio Fasano, M.D., director of the Center for Celiac Research at Massachusetts General Hospital in Boston. Unless you have celiac disease or a true gluten sensitivity, there's no clear medical reason to eliminate it, Fasano says. In fact, you might be doing your health a disservice.

"When you cut out gluten completely, you can cut out foods that have valuable nutrients," he says, "and you may end up adding more calories and fat into your diet." Before you decide to ride the wave of this dietary trend, consider why it might not be a good idea.

1. Gluten-Free Isn't More Nutritious (and May Be Less So)

A quarter of the people in our survey thought gluten-free foods have more vitamins and minerals than other foods. But a recent Consumer Reports review of 81 products free of gluten across 12 categories revealed that they're a mixed bag in terms of nutrition. "If you go completely gluten-free without the guidance of a nutritionist, you can develop deficiencies pretty quickly," warns Laura Moore, R.D., a dietitian at the University of Texas Health Science Center at Houston. Many gluten-free foods aren't enriched or fortified with nutrients such as folic acid and iron; the products that contain wheat flours are.

If you don't have to give up gluten, the likelihood that you'll consume a significant amount of arsenic following a typical gluten-free diet should give you pause.

And it may come as a surprise to learn that ditching gluten often means adding sugar and fat. "Gluten adds oomph to foods—wheat, rye, and barley all have strong textures and flavors," says Angela Lemond, a registered dietitian nutritionist in Dallas and a spokeswoman for the Academy of Nutrition and Dietetics. Take it out of food that usually contains it and you might find that extra fat, sugar, or sodium have been used to compensate for the lack of taste. For example, the Walmart regular blueberry muffins we looked at had 340 calories, 17 grams of fat, and 24 grams of sugars. Gluten-free blueberry muffins from Whole Foods had 370 calories, 13 grams of fat, and 31 grams of sugars. Thomas' plain bagels had 270 calories and 2 grams of fat; Udi's plain gluten-free bagels had 290 calories and 9 fat grams. We found similar differences in all 12 food categories. It may not seem like much, but a few grams here and there can add up. A gluten-free bagel for breakfast and two slices of gluten-free bread at lunch means 10 to 15 additional grams of fat.

Gluten may actually be good for you. There's some evidence that the protein has beneficial effects on triglycerides and may help blood pressure. The fructan starches in wheat also support healthy bacteria in your digestive system, which in turn may reduce inflammation and promote health in other ways. One small study found that healthy people who follow a gluten-free diet for a month have significantly lower levels of healthy bacteria.

2. You'll Probably Increase Your Exposure to Arsenic

About half of the gluten-free products Consumer Reports purchased contained rice flour or rice in another form. In 2012 we reported on our tests of more than 60 rices and packaged foods with rice (such as pasta, crackers, and infant cereal). We found measurable levels of arsenic in almost every product tested. Many of them contained worrisome levels of inorganic arsenic, a carcinogen. We've done more testing to see whether there are some types of rice we can recommend as lower in arsenic than others, and whether other grains (gluten-free ones like quinoa as well as bulgur and barley) contain significant levels of arsenic. We've also done additional analyses of data from the Food and Drug Administration to determine arsenic levels in packaged foods that have rice.

A 2009–10 study from the Environmental Protection Agency estimates that 17 percent of an average person's dietary exposure to inorganic arsenic comes from rice. That may be an underestimate, especially for people on a gluten-free diet. It's getting easier to find gluten-free foods that don't contain rice, but the majority of them do. "If you don't have to give up gluten, the likelihood that you'll consume a significant amount of arsenic following a typical gluten-free diet should give you pause," says Michael Crupain, M.D., M.P.H., associate director of Consumer Safety and Sustainability at Consumer Reports. In a 2014 Spanish study, researchers estimated the arsenic intake of adults with celiac disease. They devised a daily menu that assumed someone would eat rice or a rice product high in arsenic at every meal and snack. A 128-pound woman following such a diet would get 192 micrograms of inorganic arsenic per week from rice and rice foods alone. For a man weighing 165 pounds, it would be 247 micrograms. "These levels are close to 10 times the amount of inorganic arsenic we think consumers should get in their diets on a weekly basis," Crupain says.

Our research found that in every category except ready-to-eat cereal, the gluten-free versions were more expensive than their regular counterparts.

---

3. You Might Gain Weight

More than a third of Americans think that going gluten-free will help them slim down, according to our survey. But there's no evidence that doing so is a good weight-loss strategy; in fact, the opposite is often true. In a review of studies on nutrition and celiac disease published in the *Journal of Medicinal Food*, researchers said that a gluten-free diet "seems to increase the risk of overweight or obesity." The authors attributed that to the tendency for gluten-free foods to have more calories, sugars, and fat than their regular counterparts.

People who have celiac disease often gain weight when they go gluten-free, Fasano notes. That's because the damage gluten does to their small intestine prevents them from digesting food properly. Their digestive system heals after they have given up gluten and they're able to absorb key vitamins and nutrients from the foods they eat, including calories. In a study of 369 people with celiac disease, 42 percent of those who were overweight or obese lost weight after almost three years on a gluten-free diet, but 27 percent of them gained weight. In another study, 82 percent of those who were overweight at the start of it gained weight.

What about those who say they got rid of their belly when they ditched the wheat? There's no evidence that it was due to cutting gluten. "If people lose weight on a gluten-free diet, it might be because they're cutting calories, eating less processed food or sweets, or cutting portions of starchy foods like pasta and bread," says Samantha Heller, R.D., senior clinical nutritionist at NYU [New York University] Langone Medical Center. "Instead of a cookie, they're eating an apple. Instead of pasta, they're eating a high-fiber, gluten-free whole grain like quinoa. Eating more fiber helps satiety and may aid in weight loss."

4. You'll Pay More

Our research found that in every category except ready-to-eat cereal, the gluten-free versions were more expensive than their regular counterparts, about double the cost, and in some cases considerably more. For example, brownies made from the Duncan Hines regular mix cost about 8 cents per serving; Betty Crocker's gluten-free mix cost 28 cents per serving. The per-serving cost of Nabisco's Multigrain Wheat Thins is 31 cents; it's 57 cents for the company's gluten-free Sea Salt & Pepper Rice Thins. DiGiorno's Pizzeria Four Cheese frozen pizza is $1.38 per serving; Freschetta's Gluten Free Thin & Crispy Four Cheese frozen pizza is $2.50 per serving.

Why are foods without gluten more expensive? "One factor in the price differential may be attributed to the added costs incurred by the manufacturer to meet certification and labeling regulations," explains Andrea Levario, executive director of the American Celiac Disease Alliance, a nonprofit group.

5. You Might Miss a Serious Health Condition

If you're convinced that you have a problem with gluten, see a specialist to get a blood test to check for certain antibodies associated with celiac disease. You need to be eating gluten when the test is done to get a proper diagnosis, notes Peter Green, M.D., director of the Celiac Disease Center at Columbia University's medical school. If it's positive, then you should have an endoscopic biopsy of your small intestine to check for damage.

Your symptoms may also be a reaction to something other than gluten in your diet. "We commonly see patients who go on a gluten-free diet and feel better for a week or two," explains Joseph Murray, M.D., a gastroenterologist at the Mayo Clinic. "It may be the placebo effect or simply because they're eating less. For some, their symptoms come back, so they decide to drop another food group, and then a few weeks later, when they're still not feeling any better, they make an even more drastic change, like going completely vegan. By the time they enter my office, they're on a severely restricted diet and still have symptoms." The reason? It often turns out their condition wasn't celiac disease or even gluten sensitivity at all, but another condition, such as irritable bowel syndrome.

For people with celiac disease, inaccurate claims can be damaging. As always, it's best to read the ingredients list.

Some people may benefit from something called the low-FODMAPs diet. The acronym stands for fermentable oligo-dimonosaccharides and polyols. They're the carbohydrates fructose (found in fruit and honey); lactose (in dairy); fructans (in wheat, garlic, and onions); galactans (in legumes) and polyols (sugar-free sweeteners); and stone fruit like apricots, cherries, and nectarines. The diet is complicated, however, and you might need to work with a GI [gastrointestinal] specialist or nutritionist to help you figure out which foods to eat.

6. You Might Still Be Eating Gluten, Anyway

A recent study in the *European Journal of Clinical Nutrition* looked at 158 food products labeled gluten-free over three years. It found that about 5 percent—including some that were certified gluten-free—didn't meet the FDA's limit of less than 20 parts per million of gluten. The products were tested before the FDA's rule went into effect last summer. Still, that standard doesn't stipulate that manufacturers must test their products before making a gluten-free claim. "Cross-contamination can occur," Levario explains. "Gluten-free products may be manufactured on the same equipment used for wheat or other gluten-containing products." That can also happen when wheat is grown next to other grains. For example, oats are often grown in or near fields where wheat has been grown. As a result, wheat finds its way into the oat harvest and contaminates its subsequent products.

There's no way to completely protect yourself, but you can call manufacturers. "They should be transparent about what tests they use to determine whether a product is gluten-free," says the study's author, Tricia Thompson, M.S., R.D., founder of Gluten Free Watchdog. "If they insist that it's proprietary information, that should set off an alarm."

Another concern is that some products, particularly chips and energy bars, that carry a no-gluten claim contain malt, malt extract, or malt syrup, which are usually made from barley. As the study notes, "some manufactures mistakenly believe that the only criterion for labeling a food gluten-free is that it tests less than 20 ppm gluten." The FDA also stipulates that the food can't contain an ingredient derived from a gluten grain that has not been processed to remove the gluten. For people with celiac disease, inaccurate claims can be damaging. As always, it's best to read the ingredients list.

A Commonsense Way to Go Gluten-Free

If you must cut out gluten, be sure to do it the healthy way:

Get your grains. Whether you're on a gluten-free diet or not, eating a variety of grains is healthy, so don't cut out whole grains. Replace wheat with amaranth, corn, millet, quinoa, teff, and the occasional serving of rice.

Shop the grocery store perimeter. Stick with naturally gluten-free whole foods: fruit, vegetables, lean meat and poultry, fish, most dairy, legumes, some grains, and nuts.

Read the label! Minimize your intake of packaged foods made with refined rice or potato flours; choose those with no-gluten, non-rice whole grains instead. Whenever you buy processed foods, keep an eye on the sugar, fat, and sodium content of the product.

10

Insects Should Be a Part of People's Diets

Aaron T. Dossey

Aaron T. Dossey is a biochemist, entomologist, and founder and owner of All Things Bugs, a research and development company.

With a growing human population and dwindling natural resources, insects should be eaten to avoid a global food crisis. For instance, they are high in protein, with levels similar to beef and milk. Insects are also much more sustainable to raise than vertebrate livestock, requiring less food and water in addition to no grains and corn. In addition, insects require little land to be farmed in large quantities—they reproduce more, grow faster, and have shorter life spans. And because they make up the largest and most diverse group of organisms, there is an "insect buffet" virtually everywhere on earth, which can protect food security. With advancing technologies, the possibilities of eating insects are unlimited.

As the human population grows, it is ever more important to temper our levels of consumption of the Earth's dwindling resources. Humans currently consume at least 40 percent of potential terrestrial productivity, and some 30 percent of the land on Earth is used to pasture and feed livestock. Food reserves are the lowest they've been in 40 years, yet—thanks to an expanding population that the United Nations

Aaron T. Dossey, "Why Insects Should Be in Your Diet," *The Scientist*, February 1, 2013. Adapted with permission of The Scientist. The original article appeared in the February 2013 issue and can be accessed online at http://www.the-scientist.com/?articles.view /articleNo/34172/title/Why-Insects-Should-Be-in-Your-Diet/. All rights reserved.

(UN) expects to grow to more than 9 billion by 2050—the demand for food will increase dramatically over the coming decades. Climate change, reduced productivity of agricultural lands, overfishing, dwindling freshwater resources, pollution from fertilizers and pesticides, and a host of other factors mean that this population increase will place a disproportionate burden on Earth's ecosphere. Something has to change.

One possible solution exists literally right under our noses, as well as below our feet and all around us: insects. Though most Westerners often turn up their noses at the idea of eating the small six-legged creatures, these animals have numerous attributes that make them attractive sources of highly nutritious and sustainable food. In fact, two of the UN's eight Millennium Development Goals—eradicating extreme poverty and hunger, and reducing child mortality rates—can be directly addressed by expanding consumption of edible insects.

Insects can be produced more sustainably and with a much smaller ecological footprint than vertebrate livestock.

Indeed, the call for using insects to improve human food security has gotten louder in recent years. Since about 2004, the UN Food and Agricultural Organization (FAO) has been interested in the use of insects as alternative food sources. As a result, FAO has organized two international meetings on this topic, bringing together researchers, practitioners, and industry representatives from around the world to discuss the feasibility and benefits of insects as a food source: a 2008 workshop in Thailand, which led to the important book *Forest Insects as Food: Humans Bite Back*, and a technical consultation that I attended in January 2012 at FAO headquarters in Rome. While the attendees recognized that much government and industry backing will need to be garnered to support the widespread implementation of insect-based diets, there was an air of optimism that insect-based food products can realistically become an important part of our future.

Healthy Food, Healthy Environment

Animals, including insects, are important or even sole sources of numerous necessary nutrients, such as the eight essential amino acids, vitamin B12, riboflavin, the biologically active form of vitamin A, and several minerals. Insects are particularly high in protein, with levels comparable to beef and milk. House crickets, for example, contain approximately 21 grams of protein per 100 grams of cricket, while ground beef contains about 26 grams per 100 grams of meat and powdered whole milk contains about 26 grams of protein per 100 grams. Insects are also particularly rich in fat, and can thus supply a high caloric contribution to the human diet, particularly in famine-stricken areas of the world.

Eating insects instead of cattle is also good for the environment. Insects can be produced more sustainably and with a much smaller ecological footprint than vertebrate livestock. They are very efficient at transforming a wide variety of organic matter into edible body mass. For example, cows consume 8 g of feed to gain 1 g in weight, whereas insects can require less than 2 g of feed for the same weight gain. This is partly due to the fact that insects are poikilothermic, or "cold-blooded," and thus use less energy to maintain body temperature. This efficiency reduces the amount of animal feed needed to generate the same amount of "meat," cutting the amount of water used for irrigation; the area of land dedicated to growing food for livestock; and the use of pesticides that can be expensive, harmful to the environment, and pose a risk to human health.

Additionally, many insects, such as flies, crickets, grasshoppers, and beetles, can consume agricultural waste or plants that humans and traditional livestock cannot. By converting biomass that is not consumable by humans into edible insect mass, insects don't compete with the human food supply, as do vertebrate livestock such as cows and chickens, which are primarily fed with grain and corn.

When it comes to producing foods made from insects, the sky's the limit.

Insects are also easy to farm in large quantities using very little space. Compared to many other animals, insects have substantially higher fecundity—they reproduce more prolifically—and shorter life spans, so they can be grown rapidly. For example, house crickets can lay 1,200–1,500 eggs in a 3- to 4-week period, whereas beef cattle require about four breeding animals for each animal marketed. Insects also use much less water than vertebrate livestock because they obtain hydration directly from food. Finally, insects give off lower levels of greenhouse gases than cows.

An Insect Buffet

Insects make up the largest and most diverse group of organisms on Earth, with more than 1 million species described and 4–30 million species estimated, living in every niche inhabited by humans and beyond. This diversity makes them a safer bet for future food security than vertebrate animals such as cattle, fowl, or even fish, which are increasingly susceptible to disease and overharvested from the wild. Because there are insects of some sort on nearly every patch of land on Earth, chances are that some local species in every area can be caught or farmed as human food without transporting nonnative species into the area. The UN FAO estimates that there are already more than 1,400 species of edible insects currently consumed by people; other estimates put that number over 2,000.

When it comes to producing foods made from insects, the sky's the limit. Once the technologies are developed to produce insect-based food ingredients, they can be incorporated into numerous consumer items, such as meat substitutes and protein-fortified dry products, including cereals, bars, and snack foods. There is already an increasing market for insect-based food products worldwide. Some US restaurants, particularly those serving Latin American and Asian cuisine, are increasingly offering insects on their menus. Additionally, insect biomass may hold potential for high-value products such as food additives, nutritional supplements, antimicrobials, biomaterials, and more. Products made of chitin from insect exoskeletons—left over after food processing—may prove to be yet another valuable resource, possibly generating enough revenue to subsidize the insect-based food industry.

In summary, insects hold great potential to contribute to global food security. They present a substantial opportunity to provide much-needed animal-sourced nutrients, particularly to the developing world. The potential for insects to contribute to human well-being and sustainability is dwarfed only by the amazing diversity and adaptability demonstrated by these magnificent creatures in nature.

11

Insects Should Not Be a Part of People's Diets

Brian Tomasik

Brian Tomasik is a researcher at the Foundational Research Institute, an organization based in Albany, New York, that aims to reduce suffering.

Eating insects as food, or entomophagy, is offered as an alternative with a lower environmental impact than factory farming livestock. Nonetheless, it may not be humane or sustainable. In fact, eating insects involves killing much higher numbers of animals per unit of protein, which is worsened given insects' high rates of premature mortality. Farming and slaughtering them also involves pain and cruelty, and entomophagy may not reduce crop cultivation because insects need to be fed. If eating insects as food goes mainstream, it will change perceptions of them, creating greater cognitive dissonance in caring for them ethically. Instead, focus should be on developing and eating plant-based meat substitutes.

Entomophagy has been proposed for environmental and food-security reasons, particularly in the developing world.

However, the idea of eating insects for food is becoming more mainstream in Western countries as well, particularly among trendsetting, ecologically conscious consumers.

Entomophagy is already widespread in many poor countries. In this piece I focus on proposals to introduce entomophagy to developed countries, because here eating insects rather than plant-based protein is obviously a luxury, not a dietary staple by the world's poor.

Why Insect Farming May Cause More Suffering than Livestock Farming

The number of insects required to produce a single meal is orders of magnitude higher than the number of chickens or especially cows required to produce that meal. Even if we give insects less moral weight per individual than bigger animals, when we sum overall the insects involved, the total suffering to produce a meal adds up to a big amount. I suspect one reason people don't mind eating insects as much as livestock is that people picture a single insect and think, "Meh, that little thing isn't very important. So I'm ok with eating insects." But they forget to add up all the insects that go into their food, which collectively look more like a big animal than a tiny one.

While some small-scale insect farms may be aiming to avoid [the hazards of factory farming], it's not clear that in the long run the entomophagy business wouldn't go in a similar direction as the livestock business.

In addition, insects may inherently suffer more than large animals, because most insect offspring die shortly after birth, whereas most cows and pigs that are born survive. These infant insect deaths are unavoidable and can't be euthanized away. Thus, even if the insects being raised lived in the most luxurious conditions imaginable, they would still carry with them immense amounts of inevitable suffering.

Of course, this same point applies to wild insects, and this is a main reason why I'm concerned about the vast amounts of insect suffering in nature. But even if farmed insects potentially live better lives than wild insects, this doesn't make it right to bring more of them into existence if their lives are still on average awful.

Living Conditions

Some argue that farmed insects enjoy pleasant lives: "Insects raised in farms live in teeming dark conditions (preferable environment), with ample and abundant food supply, no natural predators, no risk of outside diseases or parasites [. . .]." But this ignores the overwhelming infant mortality of insects, which may be painful for those insects that die early and is an inevitable byproduct of breeding more insects.

In addition, these "luxurious" conditions could equally well be marketed to justify raising *any* farm animal, except maybe the part about dark conditions. Why don't factory farms embody this same dream of abundant food, no predators, limited risk of disease, and so on? It's because in practice, farms don't want to spend too much effort on maintenance or optimal welfare. It pays to cram animals into smaller spaces, allow disease and illness in order to cut costs, and so on. While some small-scale insect farms may be aiming to avoid this outcome, it's not clear that in the long run the entomophagy business wouldn't go in a similar direction as the livestock business. Maybe if the insect-eating demographic is more liberal/eco-conscious/etc., it would push for more humane raising conditions, but the same is true if that demographic were eating livestock. (Note that I don't necessarily think small, eco-conscious livestock farms are more humane, because their slaughter methods may be worse than at factory farms due to lack of pre-slaughter stunning.)

What about do-it-yourself insect farmers? It's hard to say for sure, but these might be worse than big farms. Lots of amateurs might try an insect farm in their basements and in one way or another cause immense suffering—whether by forgetting to water the insects, or starving them, or not sealing the container and causing an insect infestation. My family used to raise worms for composting, and the number of times we accidentally killed the whole worm batch in a gruesome way was more than one.

Slaughter

The Wikipedia article on "Welfare of farmed insects" has a helpful section discussing how insects are slaughtered—in developing countries, commercial farms, and by hobbyist insect eaters. I won't repeat that information here.

Of course, one would have to explain why promoting entomophagy is more effective at [mitigating climate change] than promoting plant-based meat substitutes.

Many of the inhumane ways in which insects are killed involve heating—boiling, frying, steaming, roasting, etc. This is probably extremely aversive. Insects have heat sensors and display avoidance in response to hot stimuli. In fact, even the simple *C. elegans* nematode (not an insect) avoids heat, and its escape behavior is modulated by opioids, just like in humans ("The effect of opioids and their antagonists on the nocifensive response of *Caenorhabditis elegans* to noxious thermal stimuli").

Environmental Considerations

The best argument I can see for entomophagy would run as follows: Entomophagy might cause some people to switch from eating livestock to insects, which would slightly reduce climate change and other environmental dangers, which would ever-so-slightly enhance prospects for a stable and cooperative future, and this is worth immense additional suffering in the short run.

Of course, one would have to explain why promoting entomophagy is more effective at this goal than promoting plant-based meat substitutes, which are already abundant and much less resisted on "ickiness" grounds. (Even *in vitro* meat is plausibly less "icky" than insects, and certainly regular plant-based meat products are.) In fact, I suspect the ickiness of entomophagy is part of the appeal for some people: It seems like a cool, counter-cultural thing to do, with much more impact to onlookers than just saying "I'm vegetarian." Of course, some entomophagy advocates do genuinely care about the cause on its merits, and I respect that stance.

One might argue that the additional grain fed to livestock requires killing massive numbers of insects on crop fields, so that the total insect death toll may be higher from eating bigger animals. This may be true, but it's not clear to me that crop cultivation is net bad for insects in the long run. In fact, growing crops plausibly prevents more insects deaths than it causes. The strongest argument against crop cultivation has to do with the far future, not with wild-animal suffering in the short run.

Finally, it's not obvious how big the environmental gains are for do-it-yourself insect farmers. Growing insects requires a fair amount of work for a relatively small output, and growers may need to buy grains/fruits/vegetables to feed the insects, though food scraps can also contribute to home-raised insect diets. More food needs to be fed to insects than what comes out, and if that feed comes from cultivated crops, it's not true that entomophagy reduces crop cultivation relative to eating veg.

Memetic Impact

A number of animal activists see one of the worst consequences of meat production as being the indirect effects that animal farming has on society's attitudes toward animals in general. When people eat animals, cognitive dissonance makes it harder to simultaneously care about them ethically. A number of studies have explored this point, including "Don't Mind Meat? The Denial of Mind to Animals Used for Human Consumption."

The same arguments apply in the case of insects. If society is going to eventually take seriously the plight of quintillions of insects in nature, it would help if its citizens didn't have a vested interest in ignoring insects' simpler but still morally important forms of sentience.

Entomophagy, if it advances in the West, would represent a substantial increase in bug products eaten by consumers and hence bug suffering.

The entomophagy movement appears to be growing at a ferocious pace in 2014. The idea of eating insects has an edge to it that makes it an attractive story for news outlets and a tempting way for eco-minded consumers to show off (even though eating vegan would probably cause less environmental impact). I'm very worried where this situation will end up.

Appendix: Shellac

Entomophagy, if it advances in the West, would represent a substantial increase in bug products eaten by consumers and hence bug suffering. Of course, Western consumers already eat trace amounts of bug products in other forms, such as carmine. Typically I assume that food additives are a waste of time to think about because they're eaten in such tiny amounts. This is probably true in many cases. That said, I was struck by a statistic about shellac production that I found worth sharing, although I maintain that eating bugs for protein is significantly worse because of the sheer quantities involved.

Shellac is an insect-derived resin with many industrial uses. In addition, it's eaten in small amounts in pharmaceutical and confectioner's glaze used on pills, candy, fruits, etc.

Most hard, shiny candies use shellac coatings. The statistic I found surprising was that it requires between 50,000 and 300,000 lac bugs to produce 1 kg of shellac. The larva are about the size of an apple seed. I don't know what fraction of the mass of a piece of candy is shellac, but say it's 1%. Then a 26-oz bag of coated candy (0.7 kg) would require at least 50,000 * 0.7 * 0.01 = 350 lac bugs for its production. 26 oz is maybe as much candy as one or two kids collect on a successful Halloween.

Now, there are two caveats:

1. Just because at least 50,000 lac bugs are required to produce 1 kg output doesn't mean that many bugs are *killed* in producing that much output. Indeed, my understanding is that many of the bugs can escape when raw lac material is used to produce shellac.

2. Even the bugs that are killed may be crushed or drowned or something to produce seedlac from sticklac, and maybe such deaths aren't worse than dying naturally. That said, it seems generally worse to kill insects before they would die naturally because this increases the amount of death per unit of life on average, which means more total suffering.

If we say that the world produces maybe 20,000 tons of shellac per year (assume metric tons, i.e., 1000 kg), and each requires 50,000 insects to produce, that's a total of 1 trillion insects per year.

When lac bugs are used to produce red dye, the process is more gruesome, because in this case, the bug bodies themselves produce the coloring. The bugs are typically left to die in the sun. Fortunately, lac for dye is less needed than in the 1700s–1800s due to artificial substitutes:

> In the dim past, shellac was harvested not for the resin we
> know, but for the natural dye I spoke of. Because true red

dyes were once very hard to come by, shellac dye (which is red) was quite valuable—vastly more valuable than the resin, which was little more than a byproduct. It was so valuable that one large shellac processor, Angela Bros., saw fit to build a huge new processing plant in Calcutta in 1855. That was a masterpiece of bad timing. One year later, in 1856, a guy named [William Henry Perkin] developed the first synthetic aniline dyes from coal tar, which for the first time in history made red dye cheap enough so that it was no longer practical to extract it from shellac.

That's great news. More good news is that there's a plant-based alternative to shellac-based confectioner's glaze: zein. Also, some candies don't contain shellac, including M&M's, Skittles, and Starburst.

Another instance of artificial materials helping to reduce the need for natural, insect-harming products is the partial replacement of silk with artificial silk and especially nylon. Unfortunately, people also continue to produce real silk, which requires steaming and fumigating ~10,000 worms per sari dress.

One other much less common use of insects is crushing Spanish flies to produce a supposed aphrodisiac. Despite historical instances of their use, crushed Spanish flies are thankfully discredited today because they work by producing a swelling rash and can be fatal in higher closes. Wikipedia reports: "The ease of toxic overdose makes this highly dangerous, so the sale of such products as Spanish fly has been made illegal in most countries."

Organizations to Contact

The editors have compiled the following list of organizations concerned with the issues debated in this book. The descriptions are derived from materials provided by the organizations. All have publications or information available for interested readers. The list was compiled on the date of publication of the present volume; the information provided here may change. Be aware that many organizations take several weeks or longer to respond to inquiries, so allow as much time as possible.

American Meat Science Association (AMSA)
201 W. Springfield Ave., Suite 1202, Champaign, IL 61820
(800) 517-2672
website: www.meatscience.org

The American Meat Science Association (AMSA) is an individual membership organization of more than one thousand meat scientists representing major university research and teaching institutions and meat processing companies in the United States and internationally. Its members conduct basic and applied research and education programs in muscle growth and development, meat quality, food safety, processing technology, and consumer and marketing issues relevant to the international meat industry. AMSA publishes the *Meat Science Journal*.

American Nutrition Association (ANA)
PO Box 262, Western Springs, IL 60558
(708) 246-3663
website: http://americannutritionassociation.org

A nonprofit, the American Nutrition Association (ANA) began in 1972 as the Nutrition for Optimal Health Association (NOHA). Its mission is to promote optimal health through nutrition and wellness education. With science-based nutrition, ANA educates both laypeople and professionals about the health benefits of nutrition and wellness. It publishes a newsletter, *Nutrition Digest*, and offers information on health issues and nutrition at the ANA website.

Environmental Working Group (EWG)
1436 U St. NW, Suite 100, Washington, DC   20009
(202) 667-6982
website: www.ewg.org

The Environmental Working Group (EWG) is a nonprofit, nonpartisan organization dedicated to protecting human health and the environment. Its goal is to educate and empower consumers to make safer and more informed decisions about the products they buy and the companies they support. With the EWG Food Scores app, it helps consumers rate the nutrition, ingredient, and processing concerns of foods while they shop.

European Food Information Council (EUFIC)
Tassel House, Paul-Emile JANSON 6, Brussels   1000
   Belgium
e-mail: eufic@eufic.org
website: www.eufic.org

Founded in 1995, the European Food Information Council (EUFIC) is a nonprofit organization that aims to help better inform consumers in choosing well-balanced, safe, and healthy eating habits and lifestyle. It offers publications on food issues and a newsletter, *Food Today*, online.

Food and Agriculture Organization of the United Nations (FAO)
Viale delle Terme di Caracalla, Rome   00153
   Italy
(+39) 06 57051
e-mail: FAO-HQ@fao.org
website: www.fao.org

The three main goals of the Food and Agriculture Organization of the United Nations (FAO) are the eradication of hunger, food insecurity, and malnutrition; the elimination of poverty and the driving forward of economic and social progress for all; and the sustainable management and utilization of natural resources, including land, water, air, climate, and genetic resources for the benefit of present and future generations. FAO's Fisheries and Aquaculture Department works toward the sustainable use of fisheries and aquaculture resources to contribute to human well-being, food security, and poverty alleviation.

Organic Consumers Association (OCA)

6771 South Silver Hill Dr., Finland, MN 55603
(218) 226-4164 • fax: (218) 353-7652
website: www.organicconsumers.org

The Organic Consumers Association (OCA) is an online and grassroots nonprofit public interest organization campaigning for health, justice, and sustainability. The OCA deals with crucial issues of food safety, industrial agriculture, genetic engineering, children's health, corporate accountability, fair trade, environmental sustainability, and other key topics. It is the only organization in the United States focused exclusively on promoting the views and interests of the nation's estimated fifty million organic and socially responsible consumers.

US Department of Agriculture (USDA)

1400 Independence Ave. SW, Washington, DC 20250
(202) 720-2791
website: www.usda.gov

The US Department of Agriculture (USDA) aims to expand economic opportunity through innovation, helping rural America to thrive; to promote agriculture production sustainability that better nourishes Americans while also helping feed others throughout the world; and to preserve and conserve the nation's natural resources through restored forests, improved watersheds, and healthy private working lands. The USDA website covers topics such as food and nutrition and organic agriculture.

Whole Grains Council
Oldways, 266 Beacon St., Boston, MA   02116
(617) 421-5500 • fax: (617) 421-5511
website: http://wholegrainscouncil.org

The Whole Grains Council is a nonprofit consumer advocacy group working to increase consumption of whole grains for better health. The Council's many initiatives include encouraging manufacturers to create delicious whole grain products, helping consumers find whole grain foods and understand their health benefits, and helping the media write accurate, compelling stories about whole grains. On its website, it offers information on gluten and gluten-free diets.

World Health Organization (WHO)
Ave. Appia 20, Geneva 27   1211
    Switzerland
(+41) 22 791 21 11 • fax: (+41) 22 791 31 11
e-mail: info@who.int
website: www.who.int

The World Health Organization (WHO) is the directing and coordinating authority for health within the United Nations (UN) system. It is responsible for providing leadership on global health matters, shaping the health research agenda, setting norms and standards, articulating evidence-based policy options, providing technical support to countries, and monitoring and assessing health trends. Online, WHO provides information on nutrition, diet, and nutritional disorders.

Bibliography

Books

Maria Finn — *The Whole Fish: How Adventurous Eating of Seafood Can Make You Healthier, Sexier, and Help Save the Ocean.* Seattle: Amazon Digital Services, 2012.

Peter Laufer — *Organic: A Journalist's Quest to Discover the Truth Behind Food Labeling.* Guilford, CT: Lyons Press, 2014.

Elliot Long — *Eating Insects: Eating Insects as Food.* Dublin, Ireland: IMB Publishing, 2013.

Jax Peters Lowell — *The Gluten-Free Revolution: Absolutely Everything You Need to Know About Losing the Wheat, Reclaiming Your Health, and Eating Happily Ever After.* New York: Henry Holt and Company, 2015.

Daniella Martin — *Edible: An Adventure into the World of Eating Insects and the Last Great Hope to Save the Planet.* Boston: New Harvest/Houghton Mifflin Harcourt, 2014.

Patrick Martins and Mike Edison — *The Carnivore's Manifesto: Eating Well, Eating Responsibly, and Eating Meat.* New York: Little, Brown and Company, 2014.

Victoria Moran and Adair Moran — *Main Street Vegan: Everything You Need to Know to Eat Healthfully and Live Compassionately in the Real World*. New York: Jeremy P. Tarcher/Penguin, 2012.

Michael Moss — *Salt Sugar Fat: How the Food Giants Hooked Us*. New York: Random House, 2013.

Michael Pollan — *The Omnivore's Dilemma: The Secrets Behind What You Eat*. New York: Dial Books, 2009.

Maria Rodale — *Organic Manifesto: How Organic Farming Can Heal Our Planet, Feed the World, and Keep Us Safe*. New York: Rodale, 2010.

Eric Schlosser and Charles Wilson — *Chew on This: Everything You Don't Want to Know About Fast Food*. Boston: Houghton Mifflin Co., 2006.

Vaclav Smil — *Should We Eat Meat? Evolution and Consequences of Modern Carnivory*. New York: Wiley-Blackwell, 2013.

Periodicals and Internet Sources

Mary Ann Binnie et al. — "Red Meats: Time for a Paradigm Shift in Dietary Advice," *Meat Science*, November 2014.

Michael Casey — "Bugs in Your Protein Bar: Are Edible Insects the Next Food Craze?," *Fortune*, July 18, 2014.

David Ewan
Duncan

"How to Tell If You're Poisoning Yourself with Fish," *Discover*, April 2009.

K. Aleisha Fetters

"Will Going Organic Help You Lose Weight?," *U.S. News & World Report*, March 13, 2015.

David H.
Freedman

"How Junk Food Can End Obesity," *Atlantic*, July/August 2013.

Lauren Geertsen

"10 Reasons Why I'll Never Be Vegan," Empowered Sustenance, October 13, 2014. http://empoweredsustenance.com.

Caty Gulli

"The Dangers of Going Gluten-Free," *Maclean's*, September 10, 2013.

Melanie Haiken

"The Next Miracle Superfood: Insects, Scientists Say," *Forbes*, July 11, 2014.

Colleen Holland

"How I Became a Healthy Vegan," *VegNews*, December 31, 2013.

Arwa Lodhi

"The Dangers of Sugar: How Sugar is Killing You," *Eluxe Magazine*, November 1, 2014. http://eluxemagazine.com.

Melinda Wenner
Moyer

"Organic Schmorganic," *Slate*, January 28, 2014. www.slate.com.

Elizabeth
Rosenthal

"Another Side of Tilapia, the Perfect Factory Fish," *New York Times*, May 2, 2011.

Julia Llewellyn   "The Great Gluten-Free Scam,"
Smith   *Telegraph*, December 30, 2014.

Paul Solotaroff   "In the Belly of the Beast," *Rolling
                        Stone*, December 10, 2013.

Michael Specter   "Against the Grain," *New Yorker*,
                        November 3, 2014.

Honor Whiteman   "Sugar: Should We Eliminate It From
                        Our Diet?," *Medical News Daily*,
                        January 15, 2015.
                        www.medicalnewsdaily.com.

Index